USE YOUR POWER
Recent Words from Jesus Christ

F. deSales Kellick

with Dea McAuliffe

Use Your Power
© 2016 F. deSales Kellick
All rights reserved.

All rights reserved. No part of this book may be reproduced in any form, except for the inclusion of brief quotations in a review, without permission in writing from the author or publisher.

ISBN-13: 978-1530349722
ISBN-10: 1530349729
Also available in eBook

Cover Design: Elizabeth E. Little, Hyliian Graphics, www.hyliian.deviantart.com
Cover Image Credit: © www.123rf.com/profile_swevil

PUBLISHED IN THE UNITED STATES OF AMERICA

A WORD FROM...
Msgr. J. Patrick Keleher
Newman Center Director
University at Buffalo

Persuaded to make her conversations with Jesus public, deSales Kellick has given us his words - written in italics in the text - as a gift. Personal revelations such as these are seldom as clear and filled with relief, encouragement and hope, grounded in compassion or expressed in love.

USE YOUR POWER is a perfect reflection of the availability of Spirit resourced in the day-to-day. Stories of marriage, of family, children and grandchildren, interspersed with words of Jesus "scribed" by the author, reassure and challenge the contemporary World citizen to an enlightenment of grace - a recognition.

Attentive to the present situation in every aspect of the planet, we are reminded that *"It requires very little time and energy to make a difference in someone's life, yet it accomplishes more good than we can imagine."*

It grows our hope to ***"always be open to the impossible - even world peace."***

~ Msgr. J. Patrick Keleher

TABLE OF CONTENTS

1	An Early Gift	1
2	My Surprise My Gratitude	3
3	His Directions to Me	9
4	Is it Too Late?	15
5	WW III? It's Our Call	19
6	Leaders	21
7	Can You Say "Power"?	28
8	Prayer Tips from Jesus	34
9	Just Love	39
10	Dire Warnings	45
11	The Past Hurts … Let It Go	47
12	Corporate Greed	52
13	The Middle East	58
14	Congress	63
15	Judging Others & Yourself	67
16	Our Brother's Keeper	72
17	Disruptions and Suffering	76
18	Mother Earth	82

19	A Frightening Future	87
20	Jesus Says It's Simple	89
21	Brooms and the Works of Mercy	92
22	Churning Out Service	96
23	Help Yourself to Miracles	98
24	Politics	102
25	Materialism	107
26	Exclude No One	110
27	It's Not Impossible	114
28	Bad News & Good News	117
29	Take a New Look	122
30	Pray Without Ceasing	125
31	Peace - Any Hope?	129
	Addendum	133
	About My Name *(Everyone asks)*	135
	Acknowledgments – Many Thanks	136
	Appendix	137

1 AN EARLY GIFT

Many years ago, my second-grade teacher, Sister Teresa, was preparing us for our first Holy Communion. She said it would be the happiest day of our life.

Well, I wasn't so sure.

I knew I was happiest when my mother made ice cream cones for us, or when my father pushed me on the swing. Or the time our family went on a picnic and my mother frosted her pretty cake with light green icing.

But I'll be darned! Sr. Teresa was right. When I received the Eucharist, I felt ecstatic. I knew that I took Jesus right into my heart where I could talk to Him any time I wanted to. So I did that a lot.

In our preparation, Sister told us about Jesus coming back to see His friends after He died. I knew then that He was 100% dependable.

I had no way of knowing that the other children probably didn't *see* Jesus in their minds like I did, or experience the same intense feelings. I am grateful that I was blessed with insights that went well beyond the happiness of wearing a pretty white dress, and getting dollar bills from the relatives at my party.

੩✎ら

Loving another does not mean loving another's decisions or behavior

2 MY SURPRISE MY GRATITUDE

I am grateful to the Source of this book, for the amazing gift I have been given.

For years, I have been scribing words – first from my deceased husband Jack, and then from Jesus Christ. I've filled a huge stack of notebooks. Jesus directed me to produce a book filled with His words of love for each of us - the absolutely crucial need of prayer from you and from me - and warnings of severe disaster to come.

A Mystery

It began the night I woke to a blast of music. I was alone in the home I had shared with my late husband, Jack. The sound was coming from a radio in the living room. I ran to turn it off, wondering all the way who or what had turned it on. After a restless night I tried to forget the whole thing. But then it happened the next afternoon and again the next. When I came home from work and sat down with a cup of tea, the radio blared. I ruled out crossed wires and power interruptions – but I really didn't have a clue. Things were getting strange.

Jack had deep faith, having had several years of grounding in Carmelite spirituality early in life. He deeply understood contemplation and the power of prayer, and we both understood the importance of daily meditation. We read widely from spiritual literature, re-reading the Bible along with gems from yesteryear and yesterday. (see Appendix)

We both came from large families and shared a full and happy life with four kids, eight grandchildren and various pets. We had our share of problems, but none great enough to run the wheels off the track. We shared an abiding love.

Occasionally, we had talked about life after death and wondered if we would be able to communicate with each other after one of us died. Could this be it? Was there a contact? I felt so sure of the answer I turned off the radio, sat quietly, opened a notebook and picked up my pen. The writing flowed without any conscious thought from me. I simply wrote Jack's words as I heard them in my mind.

"I'm glad you are open to this – to talking with – or listening to me," he said in a soundless voice. I smiled through the tears as I wrote. He talked about our children and grandchildren, how he loved them, the paths they are on. It seemed this proud Dad/Grandpa was sitting right there with me.

"I wasn't ready to leave you," he said. "There was so much more to say and do, but I'm content here. It's like continual sunshine – everything is good – no worries. I still enjoy watching my grandchildren. In your heart of hearts you know I'm not gone and we are not separated. The veil is very thin indeed."

Within a few weeks, Jack's voice was replaced by a different one. This calm voice assured me He is my Brother - Jesus Christ. He told me to put aside all doubts and that we would meet daily when I would take a break and slow down from life's busy routines. It seems I am part of a network of scribes.

All Jesus' words are in italics in this book. Jack's words are in quotation marks.

You are part of a very large team – in many countries – that is charged with doing what you can to change the direction that humankind is headed in. We begin with blessing EVERYONE and forgiving EVERYONE. (His emphasis.) *You are not the decider of who is worthy and who is not. The terms sinner and saint – conservative and liberal – good and bad – are just words. Drop them from your vocabulary. Concentrate on terms like love, respect, heal, cultivate, enrich, embrace, assist, honor. As you convert yourselves to the positive choice at all times, you will feel and see a shift that is affecting the whole world.*

I generally wake up about 6 AM, and before long I begin to meditate or I read from a spiritual book. Jesus' words begin soon and I write them in my current notebook. I "hear" His promptings at others times during many days and evenings – and I write.

Jack continues to "talk" to me occasionally, mostly about family. He reminds me to worry less about them, and to turn each one over to God with confidence and trust.

"We can do more of this" (communicating), he

said, "I know you miss me, but really we are not separated."

Many times during the past few years when I've turned on the TV, it shuts off. The screen goes black. I've learned that a problem with the electricity is often used to get my attention. Various lamps in my home have shut off. I just reach for my notebook and pen. I start with these words, "I will to do the will of God today and every day." Then Jesus' words flow.

It requires very little time and energy to make a difference in someone's life, yet it accomplishes more good than you can imagine. Represent Me in your interactions with others. You are the one to change the world for the better. It is a sign of hope that countless brothers and sisters are world-changers with you.

Jesus directed me to produce a book based on my scribing of His words. He assured me that I was the right person for this job. To our surprise, He said that it was no coincidence that my sister Dea and I were born into the same family, and that we were destined to collaborate on this book.

The hour is late and people sleep. Ignore the thoughts that tell you this can't be happening or you are not the right person for this job. I will guide each step of this. When you feel stuck, just call upon the Holy Spirit for help and you will have it. You are not alone in this process therefore it will not be burdensome to you. Give me your imagined burdens and I will refresh you. I have much to say to any and all who will listen. You don't need to analyze what or how you are writing. Just open your heart and mind and allow Me to supply the thoughts and words.

It's time to share my words with others. The human outlook is frightening. It's time to bring others to awareness – and to change the world for good. Now. Not later. Now.

I write almost daily in what is now a huge stack of notebooks that are brimming with (1) God's love for each of us, (2) the **tremendous** need for - and power of - prayer **today**, and (3) unsettling words about disasters to come if humankind doesn't learn to "do unto others as we would have others do unto us."

Most of us have run into problems that seemed unsolvable. We might have shrugged our shoulders and said, "All I can do is pray about it." All I can do…? Jesus said that ***prayer power is greater than the power of the atom.*** Our increased prayer, He said, can save the world from impending disaster.

I have much to say to any and all who will listen. If I speak in your language, slang and all, it is because I want to be understood in this day and age of earth history. This is not to be taken lightly. You have been selected to do this work. Do not be uncomfortable and do not select words of your own. I will give you the words and it is your job to write them down.

Christ's words are strong and disturbing when He speaks about the grim state of our country and our world.

To describe your society as a train wreck is not overstating the situation. We see a government that flat out doesn't work, a worldwide banking system on the brink, education with elites that don't know how to "self-correct" their system, food distribution where some waste enough food to supply the starving, women and girls raped and murdered as people watch or ignore.

Jesus emphasizes the power of **love and prayer** and gives clear directions for building a better world.

Let the primary message of My book be of Love. I came into the world over 2000 years ago to teach love to those who lost their way. Their path was overgrown with fear and the fear took many different shapes, much the same way as it has today – in your time.

Words that I give you are words to live by. Consider them direct guidance for you and for many others. Surely you understand that this is the reason for our communication. I speak to many good-hearted souls who bond with the commandment of Love. Some preach with words, others by their actions. They live the counsel of St. Francis of Assisi: "Preach the Gospel at all times. If necessary, use words."

3 HIS DIRECTIONS TO ME

Take one day at a time and listen to what I have to say to you.

These notes about the scribing were a huge comfort to me when doubt crept in. Too often I wondered, "Is Jesus really talking to me?" I'm surprised and grateful that He didn't give up on me.

Put My Words Out There
Move to putting My words out in the public domain for those who may benefit from them. You will receive all of the support you need. This writing may be a viable factor in the process of saving humankind and Mother Earth. Your commitment is required. Support assured.

If We Want Peace …
If there is a desire for peace on earth, then embrace the **Great Commandment**. *"Honor the Lord your God with your heart, mind, soul and strength and your neighbor as yourself."*

What A Comfort

I was happily surprised to learn that all religions profess the **Golden Rule: "Do unto others as you would have others do unto you."**

Jesus indicates that the Golden Rule is inborn in human nature. Those who have the ability to listen to their heart have no difficulty understanding it. Notice here that the same message is just worded differently.

- HINDUISM: Do not do to another what is disagreeable to yourself.
- CHRISTIANITY: Do unto others as you would have others do unto you.
- JUDAISM: What is hateful to you, do not to your fellowman. That is the entire Law, all the rest is commentary.
- ISLAM: None of you is a believer until he desires for his brother what he desires for himself.
- NORTH AMERICAN INDIAN: In the beginning were the instructions. They are to love and respect all living creatures and Mother Earth.
- BUDDHISM: Hurt not others in ways that you yourself would find harmful.
- BAHA'I FAITH: Blessed is he who prefers his brother before himself.
- ZOROASTRIAN: That nature alone is good which shall not do unto another whatever is not good for its own self.

My Words Are Needed
Many will profit spiritually from My words. This is more a command than a wish or hope. My words are needed "out there" in a tired and weary world. A very great part of humankind is lost in a muddle of disconnected societies, blind to the possibilities of love, joy and contentment.

Great Suffering
Follow through with the scribing and organizing of My words so that they will reach others. The events of humankind in your time are difficult and monumental – great suffering for many of our brothers and sisters. Those who listen to My words and follow them will hear necessary guidance. Never concern yourself with how many will benefit from your work. That is My domain. Some people are in need of My words and are aware. Others are in need of My words and don't know it, but many will welcome them nevertheless.

I Am Always Present
I will be ever present through the process. People are so needy and problems appear to be overwhelming. Some of the messages from the notebooks will be helpful to many.

Others' Pain
Focus on the deep spiritual needs of mankind. When so few recognize the pain of so many, it is plain to see that something is amiss in their thinking and their ability to see beyond their own selfish wants. Many have My name on their lips but not in their hearts.

Open Eyes and Hearts

I ask all of you to pray for the miracle that will help people to open their eyes to the suffering of others, and consequently, open their hearts. There have been times in human history when the people were oblivious to the degradation in society. The outcome has been written over and over again in the suffering and downfall of those societies.

The tired and battered world is waiting for My words - you might say is waiting again for a redeemer. So many race around - both physically and figuratively - like mice in a maze. They need to open their eyes to what they are doing with their lives, and to recognize their brothers and sisters with love and compassion.

The Love messages will provide relief, encouragement and hope. Those who struggle with the day – to - day issues of life and family and work need to be lifted up and given reason for hope and love. It will establish in them the energy and the desire to help lift others – to facilitate a revolution that is grounded in compassion and expressed in love. Bless and forgive everyone – always. Go in peace.

As the world's conflicts take center stage on planet earth, it is time to share My words publicly with the ego-driven politicians and the over inflated opinion gurus. The masses are caught in the financial squeeze – working and sinking into debt.

Know that this book is vitally important for people you don't even know and may never meet in this lifetime. Many of the readers will find reason for hope in My words, reason to live, and reason for joy. Many will understand and take great pleasure in knowing they have a place in the family of God.

Rely on the Word of God and the promises of God's love. Know that united in prayer, with many others, you are part of a powerful spiritual network capable of great good.

Jesus makes it clear that our collective prayers are powerful enough to bring balance to the entire planet!

Your prayers have power for good that is beyond your ability to calculate. Though you cannot travel the world and "fix" things, remember your prayers travel where they are sent. Wrap the entire world in your prayers – all people of the earth. Pray for the ending of aggression and the birth of love in every heart and mind. Let love inspire every thought and deed. Drop judgment and blame. They do not cultivate love nor do they bring peace. Pray that leaders be guided by visions of justice and love. The problems and conflicts are monumental, but they are not greater than the power of God.

All people of faith must respect all believers of every faith. Peace is not born of disrespect or prejudice.

4 IS IT TOO LATE?

Some of the messages from Jesus are discouraging. They made me wonder if it's too late for us to link arms and make the changes we need in order to save ourselves from a frightening future.

Prayer X 2= Survival

Those who know Love must double their efforts in prayer. The lock-step march to the precipice must be halted if mankind is to survive on this planet.

Glimpse the Future

Many have access to, and some understanding of the power of prayer, but use the power rarely and sparingly. A glimpse of the future might encourage more to pray.

Any Prayer Will Help

I ask you to make prayer the center of your life. A simple and easy approach to a world that is in great need of love and harmony is not only obvious, it is a simple thing to do. **Any little prayer you say is critical and will be cherished.**

Jesus is clearly telling us that our world is in dire circumstances, and many leaders are ignoring the obvious. They plan for war globally and internationally. Others carry on warfare in neighborhoods and families and work places. Jesus says now is the time to take a close look at what it is that we value. Do we want to leave our children a legacy of peace? Then we have to join with others to turn the tide of destruction. He tells us we can do this by uniting our prayers with the prayers of others who seek peace.

At this very time, some of the powerful are ignoring the obvious warnings. They apply power to their own advantage, not for the good of all. Those who would rush to war are seeking their own ends, not the good of the people.

Throw Them a Rope

Conditions are very telling of the world situation and of the moral bankruptcy of many. Some are so mired in corruption that their vision is extremely dim at best. When they wander so far afield, the way is lost completely. It is for others to reach out – to throw them a rope, so to speak. The "rope," of course, is your prayer united with the prayer of many others. The Armageddon need not present itself if enough good souls wake up and pray for peace – for holiness – to take the place of power-grabbing and greed.

Appearances Follow Thoughts

Appearances follow thoughts and feelings – love spreads love and war begets war. Hatred follows hatred.

Gather as many people as you can to send out love and compassion. They can produce love in the world instead of hate. The alternative is unthinkable. As systems fail, there will come a rude awakening. Look at a short list of "disaster areas" – drought, flooding, mudslides, monster storms, disruption of the world food supply. Starvation of many is ongoing and growing.

Disasters ...

Disruption of Mother Nature, disruption of monetary systems around the world, the masses in poverty. Energy systems spoiling the land and the oceans. Education for "money and progress" - failing both students and societies. Harnessing human beings as pack animals in factories, on farms and mines that do not supply the compensation to sustain them.

Pray for leaders to rise among humankind, who can and will lead in a new direction. Pray that people of every persuasion will turn to God and change direction, change the focus of humankind. It is still possible.

Too Many of Us Are Robots

So many people are like plastic shells that have no life and therefore cannot relate to Life. They have become robots. Their insides are mechanical and their signals are electrical, but there is no heart – no compassion – no sense of brotherhood.

You might compare many in modern society with the German people who watched the Nazi troops goose-step across peaceful borders and annihilate so many innocents.

Jesus reminds us that enough LOVE and PRAYER can change the future. Let's love and pray a lot.

❧❧

Be gentle with everyone, but first be gentle with yourself.

5   WW III? IT'S OUR CALL

Jesus' words about impending war follow.

*The attention and the prayers of all are needed to stave off World War III. Without the **intention** of the good of all, by great numbers of people, the cause is lost. Pray unceasingly for world peace. Pray that those who are in a stupor caused by misplaced values come to their senses before the onslaught of disaster. The suffering will be beyond what man has ever imagined.*

The idea that preparing for war will bring safety and peace is preposterous. A child could advise the world leaders of their misperceptions.

*Humankind has perfected the "art of war" beyond what any sane person would hope for. There are **armaments more than sufficient to annihilate every living creature and Mother Earth, too.***

The tribulations to follow are monumental for those who lead into war and those who will be devoured by war. It is not impossible to change the tide, but you will have to pray and get others to join in your prayer efforts.

We are at the point where it is obvious that building bigger and more sophisticated bombs and weapons is not a viable answer to the world situation. A new alternative is needed, and Jesus is telling us that it is prayer.

He hammers home the message that He is waiting for our prayers. Yours. Your sisters'. Your brothers'. Your friends'. Your children's. Mine.

❧❧

Always be open to the impossible ... even world peace.

6 LEADERS

As for world leaders and leaders in your country, many are good people – some are misguided and others are on the pathway to soul destruction. The ego and greed that is so destructive to them brings suffering to many innocents.

If our leaders and the leaders of other countries are always preparing for war or going to war, then it follows that "love thy neighbor" is not a priority. What do we need to do today? Jesus said –**we must raise an Alternative Army of Pray-ers.** It is possible to **outnumber** the combined armies of the world **with a Praying Army.** We can do this!

The ego-centered politicians and generals and the fanatic religious leaders in any country are not guiding humankind to solutions. They are compounding the problems. They have turned away from their own moral, religious or ethical beliefs and are impotent when it comes to critical questions about the conditions of humankind. Man is capable of solving problems, but not without working cooperatively with God. Now is the time to love God, love yourself and love your neighbor.

Jesus asks us to *"pray for wisdom and true charity* (love*) in all those who govern and those who seek to govern. Spirit will take over from there in all those who truly desire to serve and to heal the ills of humankind."*

Who Are the Real Leaders?

Those who love God and neighbor and demonstrate love are the real leaders of this chaotic time in human history. History demands a rewrite NOW. The many who help their neighbor without invitation and without financial reward are the leaders to look to. They inspire the growth of goodness, kindness and compassion. They seed the growth of a genuine, caring community.

The Local Leader

I loved hearing this neighborhood story of conflict resolution. It's a mini-lesson on kindness and effective negotiating.

A couple of my Grandkids told me that "crabby Mr. Smitty" lived down the street. He'd holler at them if they ran across his grass or his driveway. He rarely spoke to neighbors, and often sat on his porch, ready to yell at any trespasser.

One afternoon, their father chose a bottle of his homemade wine, picked up two wine glasses and went to Mr. Smitty's door. Before long, the two of them were sitting together on the porch chatting and sampling wine. The kids couldn't believe it! Mr. Smitty was soon nodding and smiling to neighbors. He even lightened up with the children.

It was a basic lesson in conflict-resolution for both young and old. Jesus clearly states that all leaders would do well by choosing negotiations over bombs.

Pray for those who seek to govern with a desire to serve and to heal the ills of humankind. Bless everyone continually. Leave no one out for you are all one family – a family in need of tender loving care.

Misguided Leaders
As the leaders bait each other and play a game of chess with each other, they put all of humankind in a game of Russian Roulette. Think of your children and grandchildren. Think of them with love and hope, and pray daily that they be allowed to grow up. Place your hope in those who follow the moral code in all that they do. Pray for those misguided leaders who captain the teams of annihilation.

Out of Touch
You are not dodging live ammunition, but you are being strangled by many totally "out of touch" leaders. There is plenty of blame to go around. Are there enough prayers to reach a tipping point for good, for justice? Pray unceasingly. Spirit is listening. Come together in My Name. Ask the Father in My Name. He will hear you.

Greed Has Control
Some leaders are modeling defeat and annihilation. That is in the future of untold millions

of people – your fellow human beings. The greedy have assumed positions of powerful control. In the process, Mother Earth is being damaged daily by those who look the other way, or those who call the shots. Who loves God and neighbor as self? Surely not the millionaires and many "leaders" in governments and corporations.

Support Our Children

The children of the world have a right to be nourished physically, emotionally and spiritually. They have a right to grow up in a world without war. They have a right to education and nurturing of their talent and skills. They just might be saviors of this lost and bewildered world you live in. Support them.

We can be sure that many of today's American teenagers and college students have the mind and heart to evolve into competent and loving leaders. Many parents are doing a magnificent job helping them to realize what Wayne Dyer wrote so clearly, "We are not human beings having a spiritual experience. We are spiritual beings having a human experience."

Leader = Servant

Remember that I gave new meaning to the title "servant." Leaders must be servants to the cause of the common good - and in all of this, Spirit is the central piece, the keystone that holds society together – keeps it from collapsing. Represent Me with demonstrations of love.

Our founding fathers made it clear that it is the responsibility of the State to safeguard and promote the common good of all society.

Many leaders are confused as to what right action is. Right action will never be guided by greed and struggle for personal or national power.

Pray for All Leaders
The President and all leaders of your country need your prayers. The giants of business, industry and governments **have the potential to change the world for good** *– to wipe out hunger – to provide education and training for people from cradle to grave – to devise fulfilling work for all – to care for the sick and the aged – to seek the good life for all.*

Shameful Leaders
Comprehension of the terrible inequality between the "haves and have not's" undermines the equilibrium of nation after nation. Insensitivity concerning the poor, homeless and starving grows. It causes many to question both the cold-heartedness and the sanity of the so called "leaders." They can cut food for the poor, but they cannot cut money from their own bloated budget.

Pray for New Direction
Pray for leaders to rise among humankind who can and will lead in a new direction. Pray that people of every persuasion will turn to God and change direction, change the focus of humankind. It is still possible.

Enlist in This Army – We are sorely needed ...

Those who comprehend the situation do what they can. But they are a small "army." Millions more are needed to feed the hungry, give drink to the thirsty, care for the sick and the aged. They are needed to do the work of compassion. But they are also needed because they teach by example. They walk in My footsteps. You can recognize them by the love that directs their daily lives. They are the leaven in society. Those who build up the society are not the money lenders. Societies that concentrate the wealth in the very small minorities inevitably fail.

Look to the lessons of the Gospel – read them over and over again – allow them to speak to your heart and allow your heart to direct your action. See Me in "the other" and minister to Me.

Never exclude anyone from your prayers.

7 CAN YOU SAY "POWER"?

My presence was felt by everyone at your prayer meeting last night. Wherever two or more are gathered, I am in the midst of them. As you remember all of my brothers and sisters, you bring blessings and the peace of God to all of humankind. I, your Brother, pray with you each time you gather in My name.

I've belonged to a prayer group for years. It started with three of my sisters and me. We laughed as we realized this was a "solution" we inherited from our mother, because whenever we ran into problems growing up, her counsel was helpful, but always ended with a firm, "Well, for heaven's sake, just pray about it!"

I was astounded by Jesus' words about the effectiveness of prayer groups, large or small. There is no question about the need for many, many, more. What a difference they will make!

Lift the World a Notch

Your prayer group is the support of countless people. When you pray for people around the world you lift the world a notch – imperceptible to you, perhaps, but not to the ones your prayers have touched.

Soon there were eight or ten of us meeting once a week at each other's homes to pray for world peace. In a notebook, we write our special intentions and the names of individuals who have asked for prayer. We keep one seat empty for Jesus – a symbolic reminder of His presence.

A Force For Good
Continue with your prayer group. The power brought to bear for the good is beyond your calculation. Just know that you are a force for good that the world can ill afford to lose. Acknowledge My presence within you. You are My hands - My feet - My words. I bring the power and the love of God our Father.

There are probably thousands of similar groups, larger and smaller, in homes, churches and meeting rooms across the world. If you belong to one, know that His words were written for you. Jesus emphasizes the great need for more prayer groups. It is so easy to start one.

You Can Bring Balance
As for the situations of great concern in the world, know that the power of prayer is needed to bring balance to the entire planet. Your prayers and those of your Prayer Group have power for good that is beyond your ability to calculate. Keep this in mind and pray as you go about your tasks each day. Remember that God is love, and remember also that you are One with God.

At the close of our meeting, I provide an "off the cuff" meditation. I "see" Jesus in various settings, sometimes a clearing in the woods or on a beach, and His words just come to me. It's very much like the dictation that I scribe almost daily. If I'm absent, someone reads a page or two from a spiritual book, or the group will sit in silent meditation, or listen to a section from a meditation CD.

You Are Saviors of the World
The saviors of the world can be found in the small prayer groups who come together without judgment to pray for peace. Lay all thoughts aside and join Me in praying to Our Father - the all-knowing, all loving, and all powerful God.

A Healing
One evening my niece Mary Kay brought her friend June to our prayer group. June was battling severe breast cancer. Both her mother and sister died at a young age from breast cancer, so things didn't look good. A nurse, June realized the gravity of her condition.

After our regular prayers for world peace and special intentions, we gathered around her to pray for healing. As she listened to our individual prayers for her, she wept quietly and profusely. About two weeks later, my niece received an e-mail from her: "I've just had a complete body scan and the doctors cannot find a single cancer cell in my body. I'm convinced that the cancer left my body that night at your prayer meeting."

Today, June is a healthy, active nurse who visits breast cancer support groups from time to time. When a young woman with children asked her how she was cured, her gentle reply was, "I was not cured. I was healed."

Not a Random Gathering

The prayer group is not a random gathering. You were gathered together to help and love each other so that you can extend blessings and prayer beyond your group to heal others and to heal the world.

Guided by Spirit

I am always with you. I hear the prayers of your heart. You are never alone. The prayer group is being guided by Spirit. Continue to meet and continue to host those who are in need of healing. It does not matter what kind of healing is needed.

Leave No One Out

Pray for everyone. Pray for the spineless leader as you pray for the hungry child, the lonely elderly, and the struggling youth on the edge of adulthood and confused by the empty spirited and greedy society he or she is immersed in. **The power of our Heavenly Father is greater by far than the sum of the power of all the armies of the history of mankind.**

You Have the Power

You, and others like you in many lands, have the grace and the power to bring peace to all people on earth. You have the power and love of God to back you up in each and every prayer, good thought and compassionate act.

Give Prayer Your Energy
When you meet with your Prayer Group, you pray in My presence. Gift the people of the world with prayers for peace. Let your energy be consumed in prayer, not politics.

Maximal Power
The power of the prayer group is maximal whether two are gathered together or many. Continue to meet and continue to praise, ask, and thank your loving God. (I use this reminder: **PAT = Praise, Ask, Thank**)

Will you start a small prayer group? It takes no magic formula to devise a routine you'll be comfortable with. Just get together with a few like-minded friends. Choose favorite prayers from childhood, or choose selections from one of the many prayer books available, pray a rosary, or read the parables and discuss the real messages they impart. Whatever you choose will be pleasing to God. There is no "right" way to do this and no one has a monopoly on God and how to talk to Him.

Sacred Books of all the great religions speak of critical situations turned into victories through Divine Intervention. Is the Divine waiting for a critical mass of us to raise our voices in prayer?

No question about it.

The only time we have

is NOW.

8 PRAYER TIPS FROM JESUS

Scattered throughout my notebooks are many direct tips about prayer. I hope they will help you as much as they help me.

I must confess that Jack and I had a problem with this first one: *Settle into daily prayer and meditation in the morning.*

When our four kids were in school and Jack and I were both working, it wasn't possible to "settle into prayer and meditation in the morning." Too many mornings went like this: showers, breakfasts, "What'll I wear?" "Where's my math book?" "It's his turn to take the dog out," and "Turn off the coffee pot."

But we decided that God understood this, so when our feet hit the floor in the morning, we thanked Him, we made the **intention** to acknowledge God's presence throughout the day, and asked His protection as our family's day unfolded. In our circumstances, however busy, we realized we could *still* make prayer our constant companion.

None of Christ's tips about prayer involved hours spent on our knees. *"Just a few whispered thoughts,"* He said, *"will do more good than you can imagine or calculate."*

Be Consistent

Consistency is critical to prayer life. Set your schedule, your "program" of prayer and follow it each day. It opens opportunities for great blessings and spiritual growth. Pray and turn it over to Me. Stay centered and peaceful. Have confidence that help is at hand though it may differ from what you believe it "should be". Trust that Spirit sees the whole picture through loving eyes and responds. Trust that "God's good" is more powerful, complete and beneficial than anything you might choose. Always extend love through your thoughts and your prayer. Whatever you do today, make it your gift to God.

Make It Personal

The need for prayer is beyond your ability to calculate it. There are many signs in all cultures of the world that humankind is in dire need of healing, of accepting that all need to cultivate a personal relationship with God our Father. Pray as often as you can. Each small prayer is honored. Always turn to Spirit – a steady, sure guide.

A Source of Joy

Open your heart to love and your mind to learning in every situation. Be open to the Spirit in all you do. Spirit is the Source of wisdom. Be kind. The needy ones tax patience. A kind word can lift the spirit of the needy one. Make every effort to be aware of the presence of Spirit in your life. Spirit is your guide – your life map – and source of joy.

You understand the words; you must believe them. I will not leave you wanting. My desire is to give you the kingdom. Accept it. Your prayer is heard and recorded on my heart. Allow the future to open in the fullness of My love.

Like other parents and grandparents, I pray for the young ones who are facing problems. Then I leave it in God's hands. At least I try to. Sometimes I take the problem back and start worrying all over again. That's not faith, and not what God wants me to do. Jesus said:

It is good to care about family and friends who struggle with the cares of life. Pray for them, console them, BUT then turn them over to Me. I carry them to the presence of God to experience the healing love of God. Experience tells you that My healing love can and will lift them out of troubles and despair. On the other side of darkness is my healing light – it is the presence of love – it is healing made real.

Your Children
Release all of your children to My care – and leave them with Me. Sorrow, worry, stewing over past and future is not only a waste of time, it gets in the way of healing and peace. Cluttering your kids'

channels of good flowing to them is never helpful. When problems and difficulties crop up for them, remind yourself that great lessons are learned as they work out their solutions - just as you did on many occasions. The flow of life will flow easier and better for them – each one – as they grow in age and grace. No one is separate from Me. I am always available.

Get Directions
In silence and in peace ask for direction. Do not allow the violence of an unkind thought or rash judgment to disturb your mind. Remind yourself that there is only love, and the absence of love creates pain.

Peace Is In the Quiet Spaces
You will find peace within in the quiet spaces every day. Cultivate the spaces, especially the early morning. You will find me in the freshness of the quiet dawn. Order in your day provides spaces for prayer and meditation. **Always be open to the possible – even world peace.**

Prayer Beats Depression
Keep world depression and despair at bay with your prayer of confidence in the presence of God in each one and all that that implies. Go to the altar of God within you and spend quiet moments in His presence. Let your intention for peace on earth guide your thought and prayer. Time just being in His presence brings you to peace.

A Practical Last Tip
In the middle of a hectic day when everything is at sixes and sevens, take a break. A few moments with Me will smooth out the ragged feelings and put a fresh spin on things. Take a deep breath and experience My calm presence.

ಶ∞ಶ

I am always available.

9 JUST LOVE

My desire is to love you and heal you and all people. My desire is to cultivate so much love that war would be unthinkable and loving kindness would rule the day. Love is truly the great leveler. Begin with the intention to love everyone and exclude no one.

Each day on planet Earth calls for a new dedication to the good of all of humankind. It excludes no one, sick or well, rich or poor, of every place on earth. It is the time for inclusion – for accepting the idea that all people deserve space in the human family. Criticism, gossip and prejudice have no place in this family. Think of such aspects as disease that must be cured. The simplistic cure is "love thy neighbor". **There is nothing on earth that enough love cannot cure**. Apply this thought to all people and every situation in your life. When you see the results, move forward to apply it to communities, to countries, to corporations, to governments, to schools and hospitals, and yes, to skid row.

No one is outside of God's love. If that's the case, should anyone be outside of your love?

Here in Buffalo, we have an amazing island of *love* that keeps expanding in a threadbare part of the inner-city. It's St. Luke's Mission of Mercy. Years ago, after much prayer and thought, two individuals, Amy Betros and Norm Paolini, bought a closed Catholic church, a school building and a convent in a high crime area. Their goal was to bring love, compassion, mercy and service to the neighbors. They were serious about practicing the Works of Mercy. They *knew* with the Holy Spirit in charge, they *would* be able to feed the hungry, clothe the naked, counsel the doubtful, and meet the needs of many people.

Amy and Norm dropped the word "impossible" from their vocabulary. They knew that they would find a way to serve Me in the needy, and they did. If someone was asked to calculate the good that has been accomplished since the beginning, it would be beyond the capacity of the best computers.
Life is really quite simple. The common denominator is Love. Take Love with you today and spread it wherever you go.

Life is really quite simple? Hmm...But this is Jesus speaking, and here's how He simplifies it for us today:

Just love. This is not a request for a billion dollar program to be launched by the United Nations. It can start as simply as a greeting to someone on the bus, or telling a story to a child, or reading to the blind one, sharing your pot of soup with a neighbor or being a good listener. Just begin. You don't need equipment or funding or a Board of Directors. You need love.

Love Yourself As I Love You

The effects of My words, living words, in you and others, have the power to break up the stranglehold of greed, hatred, war, addictions, selfishness and despair. My words bring LOVE that establishes healing of every kind – physical, psychological, emotional – it is complete healing that I speak of, because spiritual healing is the underpinning of every kind of healing. The medicine that does the healing is Love – and that is why I ask you to not judge yourselves. Love YOU as I love YOU.

Much of Amy's and Norm's inspiration came from *The Diary of Sister Maria Faustina*, written long ago by a humble Polish nun who received direct messages from Jesus about the curative power of Divine Mercy in all situations. Her inspired words have flashed across the world, and devotion to Jesus and His Divine Mercy is found in people's hearts and churches everywhere.

Amy and Norm have learned - and taught - that love changes everything. With donations of time and skill from carpenters, plumbers, electricians and roofers, they've rehabbed local dwellings for homeless families. They feed a huge number of people twice daily thanks to support from local food suppliers. They provide clothing, love, blankets, tutoring, toys, encouragement, shoes, and more love.

Volunteers, including local adults and teens, as well as people from across the city and suburbs, keep pouring in. St. Luke's big family has learned that with Christ, nothing is impossible. To them, life is really quite simple.

Some People Are Hard to Love

Do your best to express love even when it's a challenge. Some can't recognize love. Many people grew up in angry, dysfunctional households and never experienced true love. Love is present within all. But it is buried so deeply in some that it is unrecognized by self or others – but it is there. Do your best to express love even when it's a challenge.

St. Luke's bubbles with happiness. I taught Art to all grade levels in their small school, and I treasured the warm interaction between myself and the students. Art projects brought out enthusiasm and creativity the children didn't know they had.

A Surprise ...

One afternoon at St. Luke's, I stepped into the dim, empty church to pray for a bit. I knelt at the altar rail. When my eyes adjusted to the darkness, I was surprised to see a small boy sound asleep on a stair leading to the altar. I turned around then and saw an older man kneeling about eight rows behind me.

When I left, I told one of the workers what I had seen.

"Oh," she said, "that's Moses. And that man keeps an eye on him for us during his naps." His mother dropped him off one day because she couldn't take care of him. Everyone knew his real first name, but they all referred to him as "Moses," who, in the Biblical story was found in a basket in a swampy place. The child received loving care 24/7 at St. Luke's as long as needed.

Let Joy Creep In
Whatever you do – keep Me in mind and do it with love. Let joy creep into everything you do. There is no room for trivia. No complaints about drivers – the weather – the price of tea in China. Allow love and joy space on your agenda every day.

Jesus Asks Us to See Him in All Others
Are you able to look directly into My eyes and say, "I don't care if you are hungry – I don't care if you are cold and have no shelter or clothes. I am busy. I must go shopping." People of God, you are loved. Reach out. Love your neighbor. Follow the gospel stories. Learn how to live a good life and you will not only please your God and your neighbor, you will be happy.

Judgment vs. Love
Many concern themselves with judgment at the end of life on earth. Instead, the concern might be: "Have I loved to the extent of my ability to love today?" Love is the answer to all of the problems of the world. Listen to the words of Saint Paul on

love. Read them over and over again. They are golden, more precious than jewels. (1 Corinthians, 13:1-13)

Do We Love Enough?
Mankind has been told to love one another. Further, you have been told to love the other as yourself. Look again. Does the situation of the super-rich and the desperately poor demonstrate the living out of the Great Commandment? Recall that we are instructed to "Love the Lord your God with your whole heart and mind, and love your neighbor as yourself."

The whole idea of "love thy neighbor" has been distorted or lost. If humankind is always preparing for war or going to war, then it follows that 'love thy neighbor' is not a life priority. It is not a guiding principle that the leaders or the followers hold sacred.

An effective and appreciated form of love has to do with our ability to listen - to really hear what our neighbor is expressing. St. Benedict asks his followers to "incline the ear of your heart." Nodding and making eye contact may be all the "comment" you need, but if you have comfort to give, may the person hear what he needs from you.

10   Dire Warnings

I come to you with urgent news. The upheaval is just around the corner – seismic activity will change the playing field. People will be forced to help each other. It's a matter of survival. The greedy will lose their status. Those who work together will be the saviors of your country. The "gospel of prosperity" will prove to be no more than a shell game. Get rich quick is not on the agenda. Help thy neighbor is. The Works of Mercy will drive the community to generosity of spirit.

Your country is on the cusp of profound changes. Very few will be pleased. The majority will suffer.

Precious Little Time Left

You are well aware of the need for My words. They are for the many who can hear and act. There is precious little time for meetings, plans or discussion. All manner of things are at a tipping point. Each one who has some sense of this must pray as though life on earth depended on them – for it does. Surely you know that this is the reason that I urge you to bring My words to "the public."

Some or many of them will have the vision to understand, and the commitment to pray without ceasing.

Continue Prayer Group

Continue with your prayer group. The power brought to bear for the good is beyond your calculation. Just know that you are a force for good that the world can ill afford to lose. The Angels rejoice at your coming together to honor God and He blesses your efforts and intentions.

For Your Serious Consideration

Many people in many lands follow the Great Commandment to "love God and love your neighbor," however many do not. The amount of suffering is staggering. The desire and effort to gain or maintain power defies common sense. It certainly makes a mockery of the value of a precious life – and every life is precious. When will humankind value what has genuine value: love, family, charity, kindness, compassion. Does anyone realize how close the world is to self-destruction? Does anyone care? Does anyone know what the Common Good is? Will the gigantic business interests dictate the rules of engagement that destroy the earth and the family of humankind?

11 THE PAST HURTS ... LET IT GO

You Are Never Alone

You are feeling alone, but you are not alone. I am always with you. You are burdened by the past but the past no longer is. It is gone. Let go of your hold on the past. Put your hand in My hand and trust Me to lead you to peace. The valley of darkness is no place to spend your life. When I came to live among the human family, I came to bring light. Live in the light of the grace I freely give to you. Rest assured that you are not and cannot be abandoned. You are ever a part of the family of God. I am your brother.

So many of us are haunted by past memories and wish we could have a do-over. We'd do anything to take back the hurtful words we uttered, the things we did – or failed to do. And we can't let go of the pain that others inflicted on us. Memories keep cropping up. They sour our days.

Don't Revive Old Hurts

The retention of conflict and hurt by individuals, within families, and among nations is the reason for so much of the suffering of humankind. What is gone is gone. Do not continually revive it. Let all disturbing thoughts go. Think of Me and My love for you, which is infinite.

Christ indicates that the first one we should forgive is *ourself.* Too many agonize over past failings and suffer from a depression that won't let go. He asks us to internalize these words of St. Francis deSales: *Be gentle with everyone. But first, be gentle with yourself.* Since we know God has forgiven us, the question is - who are we to waste so much of our *"now"* when we know His understanding and love and forgiveness are infinite?

Take It Easy On Yourself

Your loving Father does not judge every little blip on the screen of life as failure or tragedy or shortcoming. For "heaven's sake" and yours, do not be judgmental of yourself or of others. Think of your "heart-brain" as a source of love – not to be cluttered with opinions and judgments.

I've found that it's not easy to let go of painful memories. At one point in my life I was struggling with a *big* problem that was taking up way too much space in my head. My gut was not able to let go of the pain. Finally, I decided that if my feelings wouldn't let go, I would *will* to let go. I knew that my God-mind could accomplish things that my heart refused to do. Over and over, I told my mind, *"I will not go there anymore. I will leave it in the past and move on."*

It called for perseverance on my part but I stuck with *willing* to let go. With the help of God, I did.

Be Kind to Yourself and Others

The past is gone – is no more. This moment is the moment to live in – to care about and love others – to look to your Savior for the help you need to navigate this day successfully. Successfully means approaching every person and every situation with love and compassion. I will help you. Focus on what needs to be done with loving kindness toward yourself and others.

All We Have is *Now*

Crying over spilled milk is never helpful. Today is the concern. **Forgive yourself** *for missed opportunities and engage in the* **now**. *Negative thoughts are clutter – clear them out of your mind. Old tapes are a tangle of useless thoughts. Come home to the peace and love that I offer you. Trust Me as though you are a little child. Seek to fill all your needs through Me, your Brother.*

Divine Order

Don't look back, look forward. What's gone is gone. The only time you have is NOW. Keep ever mindful of My presence in you and in others and all about you. Know that there is such a thing as Divine Order. Rely on Divine Order. Place your trust in the infinite power of God to bring you to peace. Each day is a new beginning, so begin.

Just Begin

Dragging anything from your past gets in the way of new beginnings. Make the Great Commandment the foundation of every new beginning and the highlight of every day. "Love God with all your heart and mind and soul and love your neighbor as yourself."

You Are Precious – Jesus Said So

Let go of the past. Let go of all of it. It is not real. Go from there. The separation that you feel is simply in your mind and bound up with your feelings. Let it all go and your stumbling block will be gone with it. Your sense of separation will disburse like dandelion seeds on a windy day. Step into the peace of knowing who you are - the child of the ever loving God. You are precious beyond your own comprehension.

It's normal for us to wonder how we can "just forget" past experiences that hurt deeply. We feel injured or guilty. We hear Jesus telling us to *"Let go of the past. Let go of all of it."* Look at the first quotation in this chapter. Read it often. He tells us to put our hand in His and trust Him to lead us to peace. This is something we can *do*. Picture it. Be aware that "the valley of darkness is no place to spend your life." Let's thank Him for keeping us in His Light.

All these little thoughts are "prayer." A major message of this entire book is *prayer*. Use snippets of prayer. It's a tool to help us delete painful past experiences from our memories. Jesus says don't waste time feeling guilty or angry. Can He be any more clear? He assures us we can do it. His words will help us stop dragging negative baggage around behind us for the rest of our lives.

No More Scorekeeping

You are the gift that you return to the Giver of Life. Yes. It's time to give up your score-keeping on yourself. Exchange that for a prayer of heartfelt gratitude. You are the one who will change your world and thereby you change the world for the better. Save room for joy and celebration. Look around you and see the beauty. Let Love ooze out of every pore. I am with you. I am in you. Our love is the saving grace that all people long for. Let your love change the world today.

❧⋅❧

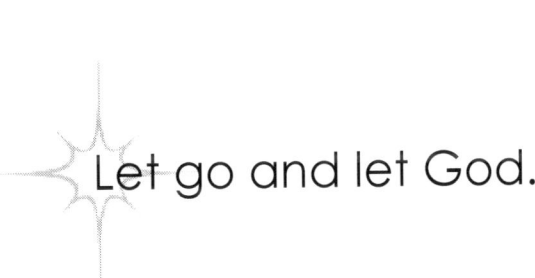

Let go and let God.

12 CORPORATE GREED

Your society is owned lock, stock and barrel by Multi-National Corporations. Open your eyes – tobacco – steel – oil – automobiles – insurance – pharmaceuticals – Wall Street and more. When you look with clear eyes, you do not see a world getting better- a world that operates from Truth, Goodness and Compassion. It is greed, deceit, callousness. Yes, there are pockets of caring, but they are not enough to change the tide of history. If you love Me and you love your family – turn to your Heavenly Father in prayer. Go into the silence and listen.

I say this not to frighten you but to wake you from the dream that life is normal. It is not normal. While the few bash the people, the land, sea and air, the sheep (the rest of us) *just watch*. While the few tend to their profits, war and disease run rampant around the world. This will not change by their "leadership." **The only thing that will alter the destruction is prayer.**

At one point in my life I worked for a large company. The managers tended to be detached and somewhat condescending. Workers' morale was low. When the "brass" came to visit the huge store and walk around, they showed little friendliness or awareness of the workers who were earning minimum wage and trying to make ends meet.

It is a given that the company you once worked for has lacked a moral guide. They are like foreigners to goodness. It is not in their vocabulary. They take what they can and they run. The lives of suffering and deprivation go unnoticed by those who are focused on profits alone. The reality is they do not comprehend what it is to gain the whole world and suffer the loss of themselves – their souls.

Popular retail giants beckon us with low prices for clothing, house wares, fast food, hardware, toys and more. Those at the executive level of these corporations take in excessive riches while those who work for them cannot earn a truly "living" wage. Many employees cannot afford a car to get to and from work and must depend on a bus schedule. They can't cover their utility bills, food, rent, medicines, clothing and other essentials.

The shift in your country in the past four or five decades has been noteworthy in its restructuring and realignment of the layers of society. The most notable is the shrinking of the middle class, and the intense poverty of the poorest of the poor.

On the other side of the coin, Jesus recognizes that many companies and organizations are made up of talented and dedicated people who serve

America well, treat their employees fairly, and earn an honest living. But His words are strong about mega-corporations and the self-serving way that too many operate. He reminds us that we could prevent a calamitous future **if we would finally and firmly believe that prayer can/does change things.**

The "developed countries" are now ruled by corporations. They own the ruling bodies, factories, the banks, and the poverty-stricken people of the undeveloped countries. You personally cannot go into these places and forcibly take over, but you can intervene with prayer.

It's commonplace in America that corporate lobbyists offer candidates big dollars if they make concessions to the corporation. Will the day ever come when we realize that corporate lobbyists should be banned from the halls of our government? It seems that many politicians lose their sense of right and wrong, good and bad, when perks from lobbyists entice them. Too many politicians and the "common good" get sucked into the quagmire.

Families Threatened

Mega-corporations are draining money from the middle class and poor at an alarming rate. Those in government who allow this - and many participate in it - are building a straw house for many families. One big windstorm will shatter them. There is no doubt that debts grow because of the immoral actions of many large corporations.

Architects of Doomsday

The insanity of many leaders, including corporate leaders, is spiraling up at an accelerated rate. There are many thousands of such companies around the world. Livelihood based on greed leads to destruction of families, companies and countries. The voice of sanity is not heard. Those in governments that allow this are the architects of doomsday.

Consider the horrendous damage caused by corporate oil giants like Exxon, British Petroleum (BP) and others. Pristine waters have been fouled. Vast fishing industries devastated. Bereft people lost their livelihoods. Waterfowl were destroyed, along with seafood that could have fed thousands. There are many dead spots in the oceans, and the gunk on the ocean floor continues to wreak havoc with the food chain.

A Sad Reality

Corporate profits rise as money is taken away from education and health care. Medicine sometimes becomes a business transaction, not a healing art. Education is one pathway out of poverty, and it will be denied to many – the money is directed instead to debts incurred by the faulty ethics of those who govern, and those who bribe them on behalf of the corporate giants.

Jesus said that if we only realized how powerful prayer really is, we would pray much more often, and we could prevent a calamitous future.

☙❧

Many concern themselves with judgment at the end of life on earth. Instead, the concern might be: Have I loved to the extent of my ability to love today?

13 THE MIDDLE EAST

 Ticking Time Bomb

The Middle Eastern region is a ticking time bomb. Each one who has some sense of this must pray as though life on earth depended on them – for it does! Surely you know that this is the reason that I urge you to bring My words to the public. Some or many of them will have the vision to understand, and the commitment to pray without ceasing.

Pray unceasingly for divine intervention in the minds and hearts of those who participate in the madness of the Middle East.

Only Prayer

You realize that the Middle East is on the brink. It is only prayer that has kept it from exploding. Some of the warmongers will begin to see that their idea will never work. They are seeing the futility of bigger and bigger bombs. All must come to the table and work things out. I will be at that table with them.

The Middle East situation parallels the story of a family I knew. There was an accidental family death that hit each one hard and brought out differing reactions. Arguments ensued. Who was right? Who felt the most pain? Who lined up with one opinion or another? Who vowed never to speak to siblings again? The questions and anger burned for years, sometimes violently and overtly, other times smoldering subtly. Some suffered serious illness. Finally, one person held out an olive branch of love and forgiveness. Others responded.

The questions changed. "Why did we allow this to break our family apart? Where is the love that was cultivated by our parents?" The act of forgiveness allowed the free expression and exchange of brotherly love. Jesus assures us that with enough love, prayer and forgiveness, even warring nations can come to peace. It is not too late if we all do our part.

Insanity

The behaviors in the Middle East are insane on every side. And they all pray to God for victory. The victory that they need is the victory of each person over his/her own life and soul. This victory will allow love to enter in after the debris of hatred is swept away by the compassion of forgiveness. Until that happens, the strife will continue. They are all mistaken in feeling they must "avenge" their loved ones' deaths.

Love is Contagious

If their loved ones could come back and speak to them, they would advise them to put down the guns and bombs and open their arms in love. Pray for a revolution of love to spread like the contagion of an air-borne disease. It will know no barriers. It will not distinguish between nationality or religion. It will infect all of them with the salvation of love. This is the way. It is the only way.

The Light Is There

You were disturbed yesterday hearing the news from Israel. Both sides are demonstrating the absence of Love. Though both sides struggle for life and for space (homeland) neither comprehends their own role in blocking peace. None can see the light in the other; therefore, none can see the light in themselves. The light is there. They just don't see it. To blow up self for victory over opponents is not victory; it is insanity. Humanity was made for greater things than war and hatred.

Greek mathematician Archimedes said, "Give me a firm place to stand and with a lever I will move the world." Jesus tells us that *we have* the lever. It *is prayer*. And it has the power to change long-standing animosity in the hearts of leaders and citizens. Jesus' words about the Middle East are clear.

Evil Warriors

The people of the Middle East are exhausted and they have nowhere to run. The same is true in African countries. Evil warriors like ISIS and Boko

Haran are at the base level of humankind. They cannot see themselves as human, therefore they cannot see others as human beings.

A strong element of evil is in their hearts and minds – cultivated in the evil of the "have" and "have not" society.

The news about mass raping, torture and slavery is shocking, horrendous, nauseating. Almost impossible to believe.

Less Talk – More Prayer

The insanity continues. Do not engage in discussion. Pray. Pray for the deliverance of people gone mad. If they loved their children, they would refuse to fight with each other. The cultivation of hatred is honed to a fine art with some of them. However, the garden produced by their cultivating has produced a living hell. This is not what the Father has envisioned for you or them.

Profits from Soldiers' Lives

As for your own government leadership – they too are marching in the wrong direction. Too many of them see profits at the expense of innocent lives of the sons and daughters, wives, husbands and fathers of those who would sacrifice for their country.

Carry the Power of God

Though you are witness to war and hostilities in the Middle East, know that your love and your acts of kindness carry the love and power of God to the whole world. Bless everyone in the Middle East, asking that God's light bring them to the truth of Divine Brotherhood/Sisterhood. Let your vision for each one of them bring their own vision to one of peace and love. The memory of enmity feeds the hostility. Pray that the dissolution of negative memories be replaced by memories of the miracle of life and the goodness of God.

※

Any little prayer you say is critical and will be cherished.

14 CONGRESS

Congress is splintered, frayed and lopsided. America is shaking its head over the stand-offs, the squabbling and lies that are constantly floating on waves of animosity. "Cooperation" seems an unknown word – too many prefer dissension, obstruction, and political rabble-rousing.

My Dad got a kick out of comedian Milton Berle who said long ago, "You can take a man to Congress, but you can't make him think." But it's not funny today.

Before the 2014 congressional elections, Jesus described the aisle in the House and Senate as *"wider than the Grand Canyon."* Our government, He says, is dysfunctional and the common good has been pushed off center stage. Budget battles, He tells us, bring deep dissension and partisanship to these non-United States. Ours is no longer a government "of the people, by the people, and for the people."

The dissension in Congress is monumental. I await the call of loving and sincere people to solve problems that are entirely self-made and self-perpetuating. Each and every person should cry out for the miracles that come "with justice for all."

Shameful Partisan Bickering

Politics is an honorable vocation, but there are too many situations that do not inspire gratitude and peace. The current stand-off in Congress is a shameful example, driven by partisan bickering. Government representatives and the giants of business and industry need your prayers. To lead and not seek the good of all human beings and of Mother Earth is to lead toward disaster for all.

Many Officials Fail

Take a look at what's happening in Washington – better I should say what's "not happening." When officials deem the defeat and annihilation of the President, or anyone, their primary calling, or the mandate of the people, you know that they have utterly failed themselves and those they represent.

A Failure to Serve

Many people suffer hardship over the lack of cooperation in Congress. Members have not admitted to themselves that they are incompetent when ideology is more important to them than the people they are to serve. Those who cannot agree have jobs with good salaries and good health care. This group has proved itself a failure in serving the people they represent.

The Middle Class

Look at the injustice toward the middle class and the breakdown and decay in your land. There is plenty to share, but greed gets in the way. It is time to drop the emotional overtones of terminology – African, Asian, Irish, Thai, Peruvian, American, Democrat, Protestant, Republican, Socialist, Hindu, Catholic, Muslim, Laborer, Professional, Domestic, Rich, Indigent, Middle Class, Ignorant, Educated, Retarded. When titles create barriers or chasms, they add to the burden of humankind.

The shift in your country in the past four or five decades has been noteworthy in its restructuring and realignment of the layers of society. The most notable is the shrinking of the middle class, and the intense poverty of the poorest of the poor.

War in Government Halls

You are a nation of warriors, and the misguided war is waged first in the halls of government. Compassion and understanding do not even get a foothold. There is a battle between factions that seek to wield power – for good or ill. **Wake up to the power and the glory of your Creator**, *not the destroyers of society and humanity.*

A Realistic Response

As mentioned before ...gathering an army of PRAY-ERS is a viable and realistic response to an impossible situation. Prayer is not an item on the national agenda, but it is the best hope for saving lives and coming to peace – the peace that surpasses understanding.

Drunk With Power
To lead and not seek the good of all human beings and of Mother Earth is to lead toward disaster for all. Humankind was not created by God for a life of misery – for selfishness, war or greed. You were made for Love - for compassion and creativity – for relationship and sharing, to lift each other up. Many in power are drunk with power and their decisions lack justice, compassion and love. Any organization or government that is divided against itself must fail. The people must demand better for themselves – for each other – for "survival."

Listen to Pope Francis
Those who govern should listen to Francis. He seeks guidance from Me from moment to moment. It would serve humankind well if all people followed his example. Wasting time brings all people closer to disaster.

Jesus asks us to pray for those who must make decisions that affect our lives. Can your prayer and mine make a difference – make our government function for the common good? Tennyson said it well: "More things have been wrought by prayer than this world dreams of."

15 JUDGING OTHERS & YOURSELF

Criticism, gossip and prejudice have no place in this family. Think of such aspects as disease that must be cured.

It's hard not to be judgmental about some people or situations. But it's also hard to find any benefit in it. A friend took a Dale Carnegie Course some years ago, "How to Win Friends and Influence People." One of the strongest points for him was the mandate to avoid the three C's: "Don't Criticize, Condemn or Complain." That's pretty equal to "Don't judge others."

Many of us claim to love God, but we routinely judge those who "irritate us" or who belong to a different religion, nationality, race, or lifestyle. Christ made this firm statement:

Do not judge anyone about anything. In the tradition of Buddha observe without being engaged and let it pass.

Our Father Judges With Love

Let your Heavenly Father do the judging, for He judges with compassion and love. Pray that all will be open to His compassion and caring. Always greet others with love even if that is difficult to do. All are members of one family – the family of God. NOW is the time for a family reunion. To bring peace, be peace.

When I started at a small college in the 1950's, bleached blonde hair was considered a sign of a cheap, loose woman. So when I met my classmates for the first time, I noticed a bleached blonde and I knew we wouldn't be best friends. But as it turned out, we saw each other every day because we were in the same field of study. In a matter of days it became clear to me that she was a gem. She was warm and friendly and had a great sense of humor. We bonded in no time. Judgment and prejudice had no place here. It was a humbling lesson and a good one.

We Seldom See the Whole Picture

Open your eyes and see that you live in the garden created by God. Do not defile the garden by holding grudges or by judging when you do not see the whole picture. Remind yourself to look through My eyes. When you do, you will see brothers and sisters who are hungry for your love and understanding.

Take It Easy On Yourself
I ask each one of you to let go - completely let go - of judging yourselves. As you do this, it will be easier for you to stop judging others. What I have to say to you will be helpful to many in their life journey. It would be worth all of your time, energy and talent if the book were to reach and teach just one person. The lesson, you know, is Love. As you let go of judging yourselves you will find that there is nothing in you but Love. I am asking you to do this because it will open the highway of My words and the blessings that I have for all of humankind.

Time to Look in the Mirror?
Never judge– it is the occupation or pastime of many, but it does not add to good and positive outcomes. Whoever judges might need to look in the mirror and seek humility.

When I first heard the story of the Prodigal Son, I sided with the young man who had stayed home and worked for his father. Why, I wondered, would a father have a big party for a son who took off with his inheritance and spent it on wine, women and song? Finally, I realized this parable was teaching us that we won't be judged sharply, or dismissed from our Father's love. We can rest assured that He "judges" us with love and compassion. Just as the wayward boy's father did.

Free Yourself
Letting go of judgment is one of the most freeing things you can do for yourself. I have said

many times that God is the only one who can judge, and He does not judge as mankind judges. He judges with love and compassion.

When you pray, include everyone, and pray for yourself, too. Let go of every iota of the past and forgive everyone, including yourself, for angry words, for resentment, for missing or ignoring opportunities to bless or help another. And while you are praying, ask forgiveness from anyone you may have slighted or been unkind to.

Not Our Concern

Discrimination and judging are not your concern. Love is. Honor God by honoring the Christ in all. Reach out and lift up with your prayer. Become healers. You need not analyze or dissect the situation. Just pray and bless. The Christ in you will accomplish the same as the Christ of Nazareth.

Don't Be Selective

Do not name the faults of others. Pray for them. Do not put yourself in the position of selecting who is worthy of your prayers and worthy of life. Each person who comes to earth has value. They have value from the beginning of life on earth and beyond. Judging is left to our Heavenly Father. He judges with perfect love and compassion. Surely, it is clear that He is the only one who sees all and loves all. Reject the sin. Accept into your prayers, the sinner.

You Are Not Unworthy

My directions will lead you to The Kingdom of Bliss. A great stumbling block for many is judgment – judgment of self and of others. It is cyclical for so many. They judge themselves unworthy and develop self-hatred. Forgive these dear brothers and sisters. Learn to love yourselves and you will be able to extend My love to others. I tell you, this will bring you great joy and it will bring union not only with your brothers and sisters of daily contact, but also with God. Do not question My words or My theology as you write. Just scribe the message – do not judge it. I come in love. I speak the language of love in your terminology. Accept it as given.

Don't Judge Yourselves

The effects of My words, living words, in you and others, have the power to break up the stranglehold of greed, hatred, war, addictions, selfishness and despair. My words bring LOVE that establishes healing – healing of every kind – physical, psychological, emotional – it is complete healing that I speak of, because spiritual healing is the underpinning of every kind of healing. The medicine that does the healing is Love – and that is why I ask you to not judge yourselves. **Love YOU as I love YOU.**

16 OUR BROTHER'S KEEPER

Whatever you do for the least of my brethren you do unto me.

Jack and I were amazed when a discussion we had with several friends led to a totally unexpected three and a half years of service. Back in the 1960's, we belonged to a group called the Christian Family Movement (CFM). The topic at one of our bi-weekly meetings concerned the United Nations and foreign aid. It seemed pretty abstract. But one fellow had just read a book about migrant workers called *The Slaves We Rent* by Truman Moore. It was about itinerant harvesters – and it wasn't pretty. We hoped we could turn words into action and arrange to help these needy neighbors.

The workers came through the Western New York area at harvest time, but we had never seen them. My friend Terri and I volunteered to make the 50 mile trip to find out more about their lives. We took our kids, a picnic lunch, and a list of questions. When did the migrants come? Where did they live? Were they families? What about the children?

We met with a priest there who was working with some migrants and knew their needs were enormous. He showed us several wretched places where they stayed when "the agent" drove them in by the busload to start harvesting. None of their scattered lodgings were on main highways. All were tucked away out of sight.

We met one family living in a tattered trailer house. They were gracious and talked about life as they tried to cope with day-to-day survival. The grandmother, who had suffered a stroke, was bedridden. Two young women, one mentally challenged, were caring for two toddlers and a boy about 8. The little ones had no diapers. There was no practical means of laundering diapers. And when we heard about their budget, it was clear there was no money for detergent!

It was too much to take in. The priest showed us some other migrant quarters that remained empty until a later picking season. Even with the cold wind off Lake Ontario, the smell of urine was overwhelming.

Discussing the needs on our way home, we knew our five CFM couples would hardly be a drop in the bucket. So we recruited others to help, and CFM groups from the Buffalo/Niagara region responded. Our kids piped up with ideas about how they could help. They were learning early on to be "their brother's keeper." The project brought great family dividends.

News stories brought a flood of volunteers, as well as donations of every stripe from southern Ontario, Western New York and Pennsylvania. Our original group became Coordinator of Volunteers, and my garage was a drop-off point for donations of furniture, pots and pans, toys, food, clothing, flotsam and jetsam – you name it.

Volunteer families gathered at the migrant site every Saturday. Within two weekends the kids had cleaned and polished bushels of donated shoes and boots. Land and a big barn were donated by a generous local couple. It became the center of our activities. Groups of seminarians and friends worked to reconfigure the barn into a dining hall, a kitchen, a clothing distribution center, and an all-purpose meeting place. My brother Jim built a pump house and we had a sanitary water source at the barn, which was now named "Madonna House."

One volunteer wore out a phone securing donations of building materials for a bathroom facility. One generous donor even delivered lumber and cinder blocks. When the migrant families arrived at harvest season, a volunteer drove a loaned school bus to pick up the children who would have been alone all day and brought them to Madonna House. Enthusiastic teenagers from a local high school prepared breakfast, then claimed a big space for working with the little ones. They read stories, played games, sang camp songs, drew pictures and laughed together. (Would you believe that the high school's name was St. Francis deSales?)

We found endless variety among both the helpers and the receivers. We were Native American, Hispanic, black, white, old, young, givers and receivers. Some of the migrant children, whose lives were continually disrupted by yet another move, had the energy and the tenderness to help a younger one, to empathize over a skinned knee, or to include one who just looked on the fun, but was too timid to join in.

We knew the Holy Spirit was leading us, and we found that the American spirit of brotherly love was rock solid. Miracles, big and small, seemed to become commonplace. This entire experience was a case of coming face to face with Jesus in many different disguises, and we came to realize it was all about practicing the Works of Mercy.

At home on Sundays we usually had a big dinner, and instead of the usual grace before meals, Jack suggested each one say what they were thankful for. Four-year-old Teresa said, "Jesus, I hope everyone has some supper."

The children were absorbing more than we realized.

17 DISRUPTIONS AND SUFFERING

The disruptions to come are far greater than those of the past. Great suffering will come to vast numbers of people. Humankind has not yet learned that harmony and cooperation lead to a life of joy and contentment. Competition based on the reach for power and greed leads to the downfall of many countries. Yes, it is possible to avert, but many people are not awake to the urgency of the situation. Accepting one another with honor and respect is foundational to the building of peace on earth. This is what humankind must seek in prayer. The urgency of this cannot be stated strongly enough.

Jesus indicates that we can avoid or weaken major disruptions if we pray and talk with Him more often. He loves each of us dearly. But it seems that many of us seldom pray. Can we change that?

A busy friend of mine told me she says, "May glory be to the Father, the Son and the Holy Spirit" many times throughout the day and she thinks "world peace." Another says, "God bless America" and "Let Go and Let God." Easy ways to "pray without ceasing."

Lay Down the Guns

The world is in dire need of turning to God for help. All of the events in the world arena are leading down the path of annihilation. Lay down the guns and embrace each other in love and peace.

Jesus has strong words about guns in America. I wrote in my notebook: "We all know that about 90% of 'we the people' came down in favor of gun legislation. Did Congress and their powerful bedfellows listen?" His response:

Your representatives will argue the new law. Is it OK or not OK to accept carrying weapons of war as a given right? To ponder the affirmative answer is the insanity of the people at this time.

Every One of Us is Needed

The world and the whole of humanity are in crisis. Turn to God, get on your knees and pray and beg for help. These problems will not be solved by a committee. They require the prayer, love and work of everyone.

A Tale of Horror

Will we ever forget the jarring TV images of suffering Syrian refugees walking, walking, walking - hoping someone would/could send help?

For days – no water, no food – fitful sleep. Such extreme suffering!

Gently wrap the refugees in your prayers. Do this every day. This world can become a haven for all – but not without the good intentions and prayers of the majority. There is no need for one-upmanship among the religions of the world. I am asking everyone to pray – in whatever language – God will hear them all.

What I have been sharing with you is for the whole population – those who can hear will hear all that I have to give. The "news" speaks of a society gone mad – random shootings on highways - literally millions of refugees seeking safety and a home - children abused and abandoned - the rich becoming insanely rich as thousands die of starvation each day. Families are selling their children in exchange for money for a few meals for the rest of them. **Work, and the prayers of all, must and will change this tale of horror.**

God will act through all those who pray and work for peace.

War Will Devour

The tribulations to follow are monumental for those who lead into war and those who will be devoured by war. It is not impossible to change the tide, but you will have to pray, and get others to join you in your pray efforts.

Effects of What Is To Come
There will be no escaping the effects of what is to come for it will affect the entire world. Fallout will be carried and settle all over the world. The volcanic ash will also cover everything. The light will dim – for many it will go out altogether. Nature run amok will be uncontrollable. Rats will carry disease. Those who are sick, hungry, lame, despondent, cold, will have no one to rely on but God. Some will, and others will curse God.

Time Is Short
I have much to say to you and to others through you. The time, in your terms, is very short. The skewed thinking is moving farther and farther away from the center, the center being My Sacred Heart. When such massive numbers of human beings, your brothers and sisters, have no clean water, no food, no shelter but the sky, no one to greet them in the morning with joy, no one to bind their wounds, no one to dream dreams of peace with, no one to care for them when they are sick or bury them when they die, then your world and your lives are so far out of balance that the blindness is almost complete.

Many People in a Daze
Untold millions of people are oblivious to the horrendous conditions and problems facing humankind. A great number of them just can't face what's happening in their part of the world or any other – going from day to day like puppets in a daze. On the international front some leaders

struggle to solve problems but others seek only more power at any cost. Look to Pope Francis for genuine moral leadership. It will not be the powerful armies that settle problems – it will be the religious beacons – the spiritually strong – grounded – dedicated leaders who will lead humankind to peace and compassion.

Choose Love or Fear

Your country is at a turning point. The same is true in countries around the world.

Choose Love or Fear. Fear is the parent of many destructive emotions and situations – a journey on the downward cycle. Love gives birth to goodness of every kind. Turning to the good is more important than anything you can think of. It is the mother of kindness and compassion. Do not delay your prayers. Talk to your loving God now. There is no other time.

☙❧

Talk to your loving God now. There is no other time.

18 MOTHER EARTH

Christ has strong messages regarding protection of our earth, atmosphere and water.

As the degradation of Mother Earth continues and severe weather conditions shout warnings of disaster – the powers that be continue to deny the reality of what is going on. The suffering will not only continue – it will grow exponentially.

The severity of effects and change will be part of the scene for some time to come. Gaia (Mother Earth) is a giant living organism that has been, and continues to be abused by humankind. Change is needed - change and caring about your mother planet. Will those who are sensitive, caring and responsible be able to support the health of Gaia in the face of the onslaught of industry, chemical agriculture, wars, mining, and oil spills?

Mankind must hold the mountains and valleys, the deserts and seas, the rocks and the trees – everything, in sacred trust. You must nurture it for your children and for their grandchildren. Be kind to your home planet, Mother Earth. This is not just a platitude. We are talking about your life support system.

Violent weather has shocked our nation and our world. People of all ages have suffered from wildfires, floods, bitter, bitter cold, soaring temperatures, tornadoes, tsunamis, earthquakes and mega storms of all descriptions.

No one seems to know that the bizarre weather is the outcome of disregard for Mother Earth. It causes severe suffering for many. Yes, there will be more weather outbursts – earthquakes and volcanoes among them. The suffering will be great –when will they ever learn?

Here in the Buffalo area, winters have often been wicked. Six feet of snow and bitter temperatures from just one early storm in late 2014/early 2015. People south of the city couldn't open their doors to the outside for days because the thick snow was higher than the doorways. And on and on it went. Forty consecutive days of below freezing temperatures. Unprecedented snowstorms crippled Boston, Chicago, Michigan, DC, parts of North Carolina and Virginia and swooped unexpectedly into other areas – often accompanied by below zero temperatures.

One night, I wrote in my notebook: "This feels like a storm of Biblical proportions. Ten to 35 below zero is the forecast for tonight. Please take care of us, Lord, especially the most vulnerable, the homeless, poor, physically or mentally challenged, young and elderly who are sick. Mother Nature is on a rampage. Snow and wind – "can't see the houses across the street."

In *Praised Be,* the Pope's recent encyclical (a short book), Francis asks world leaders for action to bring our shared home back to health. He urges us to get past the addiction to fossil fuels, and to seriously commit to other options. America seems to be catching on in many areas. For example, the President killed the proposed Keystone XL pipeline project after listening to experts who condemned the dirty oil it would carry, and concluded that it would not be the silver bullet for the economy predicted by some. Some scientists feared that unexpected consequences of Keystone could destabilize the planet.

Scientists have been talking about global warming for a long time, politicians have been talking about it for a long time, yet America's response has been mixed.

Look at a short list of "disaster areas"- drought, disruption of the world food supply – starvation of many is ongoing and growing, disruption of "Mother Nature", monster storms, disruption of monetary systems around the world. The masses in poverty. Energy systems spoiling the land and the oceans.

The poisoning of earth and air are getting close to what is called the tipping point. It's time for all people to embrace each other and work together. Begin again. Pray for all of humankind, for Mother Earth and all her creatures.

Niagara Falls, one of the Wonders of the World, became the birthplace of the electrochemical industry because of the availability of cheap power. In the early years of its development, there were no laws or guidelines for the disposal of industrial/toxic waste.

In the 1970's, good friends of ours lived in "Love Canal" in Niagara Falls, NY when it became the poster child for environmental destruction. An overwhelming number of cancers, miscarriages, and physical defects plagued the area. People saw poisonous gunk bubbling up in basements and yards, but their pleas for government intervention fell on deaf ears. Finally, Lois Gibbs, a courageous neighbor with a sick child, got the attention of the national news media and the government was forced to take this environmental disaster seriously. A massive clean-up began. The results, however, are far from perfect. We are shamed by the Native American culture that demonstrated - and tried to teach us - great love and respect for Mother Earth.

A Shameful Position

Look at those who govern in your country. Protection is provided for those who poison the earth and its waters, but it is not provided for those who will suffer great illnesses and die from those poisons.

Count On the Scientists

The scientists must devise a plan that serves humankind, and also the health and safety of your home planet - your homeland. It must be welcoming and not destructive of life – any life – people and creatures of land, air and sea.

It is clear that Mother Earth is suffering from industrial abuse. The dumpsites (now called "landfills") have the potential to make life in many areas untenable. Governmental agencies must enforce regulations that protect the people and their homes. Too many in powerful positions are indebted to each other for thirty pieces of silver.

You have been given a beautiful home that is suffering from lack of love. If all loved Mother Earth you would not be witnessing the ongoing destruction of earth, air and water.

19 A FRIGHTENING FUTURE

Your country is about to fall into a crisis beyond the imagination or comprehension of your leaders and their followers. Yes, I am saying everyone, top to bottom – has blinders on. The European nations are on the same trajectory.

Let's hope these stark words from Jesus encourage great numbers of us to pray for love and harmony in our entire world.

There is precious little time for meetings, plans or discussion. All manner of things are at a tipping point. Each one who has some sense of this must pray as though life on earth depended on them – for it does. Surely you know that this is the reason that I urge you to bring My words to "the public." Some or many of them will have the vision to understand, and the commitment to pray without ceasing.
It is apparent that the major systems of the world are failing – there are many disruptions and more to come: failing governments, education,

health/medical systems, religions, people lost and turning away, and religious leaders who have lost their way. Mother Earth is suffering – oceans poisoned, toxic air, millions of souls wandering in a desert of confusion – not recognizing the injustices and the suffering of humankind. Though they are bombarded with images both near and on the far side of the earth, still many continue to shop and pretend that life is fine – happy – good.

Many have access to, and some understanding of the power of prayer, but use the power rarely and sparingly. A glimpse of the future might encourage more to pray.

The world is in dire need of turning to God for help. All of the events in the world arena are leading down the path of annihilation. Lay down the guns and embrace each other in love and peace.

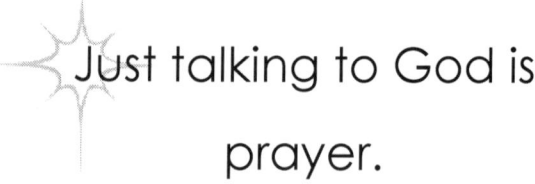

Just talking to God is prayer.

20 JESUS SAYS IT'S SIMPLE

War is not an option. Praying for peace and working for peace is the obvious answer. No matter how big it is written – PEACE – the blind cannot see – the larger portion of the population is BLIND. The first-world citizens have failed their third-world brothers and sisters. Those who seek and live the narrow life of consumerism and comfort, live emotionally and intellectually in another land.

I learned in childhood that praying was the most natural thing in the world. Even in little things. We kids never left for our neighborhood school, for example, without calling out "G'bye and God bless ya" to my mother, and we thanked God before dinner. Our family prayed together around her bed many nights, especially when my brother was in the Marine Corps.

Focus on prayer. The need for prayer is beyond your ability to calculate. Trust that this is true. I recognize the goodness in you – the power you have to save the world with your simple prayer. Do not think lightly of this. Know that one with God is a majority. ... You have pity for the one who suffers from cancer – have pity also on the one who suffers from cancer of the soul. Let go of the materialism of the "culture of more" and seek My company more. I am always present. Remind yourself of that and know that I can help you – no matter what the need is. I hold you in My heart and speak to you of the power of love. Let My love flow through you today to bless others.

Jack and I recognized many miracles as the result of our prayer. They weren't "parting of the sea" miracles, but important gifts to our family. For example, after our long experience with the migrant workers, Jack decided to change careers. He wanted to leave business for "people work" and service. That meant I would have to be the family breadwinner while he was studying for a Master's degree in Social Work. I was okay with that, and I began searching for a job.

Before long, I found a position I knew I would love. I was hired by the United Way in Niagara Falls to establish a local volunteer agency. City officials found a great need for volunteers to work with the city's youth because juvenile delinquency and crime were over the top. City leaders wanted to provide children and teens with positive, interesting activities. It gave people of all ages and talents the opportunity to help their neighbors. I was grateful to once again be in a position of service to others. I chalked up my own miracle.

Jesus asks us to work at being consistent about prayer – to find time in our days, regardless of how busy, when we can talk with Him for a while.

Consistency is critical to prayer life. Set your schedule, your "program" of prayer and follow it each day. Pray and turn it over to Me. Stay centered and peaceful. Have confidence that help is at hand, though it may differ from what you believe it "should be." Trust that Spirit sees the whole picture through loving eyes and responds. Trust that God's "good" is more powerful, complete and beneficial than anything you might choose. Always extend love through your thoughts and your prayer. Whatever you do today, make it your gift to God.

Balancing our checkbook was a problem when Jack was in his last semester. One day, we received two bills - totaling about $1000 – part for taxes, part insurance. I was exhausted at the end of a long day and it seemed like the last straw. As human problems go, this was not a major one, for sure. But still, on my knees next to the bed, I prayed, "We need $1000 and I don't know where it will come from, but I am thankful that you do, Lord."

The very next day, Jack received a stipend from the agency where he was doing his field work. It was one thousand dollars.

21 BROOMS AND THE WORKS OF MERCY

Jesus dictated…

Those who struggle for power – without love – are missing the message. The critical need now is the love and understanding of the Works of Mercy and the Beatitudes – and not in an abstract way. If they are not lived and practiced every day, the Church becomes a world organization of power, not a religion of Love. Pope Francis understands this. He is the living lesson of the gospels. He literally walks in My footsteps. Follow Him.

When I was a child, a handicapped man came to our side door every summer selling brooms. My mother always invited him in, had him wash up, and fixed him a hot meal with a glass of cold milk. Of course she bought a broom.

I learned the Corporal (bodily/physical) and the Spiritual Works of Mercy as a child in school.

Use Your Power

But I didn't fully understand just how to "do" them. Eventually, it dawned on me that my parents were regularly showing us just how they worked. The "broom man" was one example.

There are many places in my scribing where Jesus asks us to get busy **doing** the Works of Mercy because poverty, fear, hunger and despair envelop so many. Most of us can probably do four or five of the Corporal Works in one way or another. Jesus asks us - *Will you see Me in everyone you meet? Will you do these things for Me – to Me?*

THE CORPORAL WORKS OF MERCY

- FEED THE HUNGRY.
- GIVE DRINK TO THE THIRSTY.
- CLOTHE THE NAKED.
- SHELTER THE HOMELESS.
- VISIT THE SICK.
- BURY THE DEAD.

Luckily, we aren't required to "bury our dead" like the traumatized people we see on TV standing near their bomb-shattered families and lodgings. But we can give a brother a bag of apples or a jacket or those perfectly good shoes a child grew out of. We can take 20 minutes to sit on the porch with a lonely neighbor, or call him on the phone. We can donate money to the church's "poor box" or the local food drive, or a fundraiser for the homeless shelter. We have SO many opportunities to show mercy.

I demonstrated over and over the "works of mercy." They are better than any road map on how to navigate LIFE. There's no reason to complicate life and every reason to simplify life. As you do, your life purpose becomes crystal clear. That is the formula for success - Love is its foundation. Apply the Works of Mercy to the issues of your life. You will love yourself for loving your neighbor.

~~~

The Spiritual Works of Mercy

These were harder for me to understand – to put into action. When difficult conversations arise, these "homemade" translations from <u>The Message</u>, a fairly recent Bible edition, have helped me.

- INSTRUCT THE IGNORANT: Gently explain. Try to lead others to new understanding.

- COUNSEL THE DOUBTFUL: Listen with love. Reassure the uncertain.

- ADMONISH THE SINNER: Remind him or her of God's compassion and forgiveness. Speak the truth with love.

- BEAR WRONGS PATIENTLY: God loves us in our weaknesses and our strength. We're asked to do the same with our neighbor.

- FORGIVE OFFENSES WILLINGLY: This is a tough one. Choose to be merciful.

- COMFORT THE SORROWFUL: Be fully present to those who are broken-hearted and suffering.

- PRAY FOR THE LIVING AND THE DEAD: An easy one. Something like …"Thank you for Your mercy and love for everyone, living or dead."

The work before you is to love God with all your heart and mind and spirit and strength – and love all others as yourself. That is the formula for success. Love is its foundation.

22 CHURNING OUT SERVICE

The Niagara Falls job was a perfect fit for me because, like Jack, I was back in the arena of service. It seemed that all involved - politicians, volunteers and myself were actually practicing "works of mercy." City leaders tackled the crime/delinquency problems with gusto. Publicity from our office and the *Niagara Gazette* generated a big influx of volunteers. I interviewed countless applicants and enjoyed some of the best conversations of my life. During our first year, many of the volunteers made comments like this one: "It seems like God's really into this volunteer thing!"

As you seek to reach out and help communities you will find willing helpers who are grounded in love and caring. Their desire to serve inspires others and cultivates compassion. Love blossoms no matter the background or talent. Everyone will be helping someone, and the lessons of love come full-circle.

Each of the five city neighborhoods had its own core of leaders and some helpers. We added volunteers for coaching sports, teaching chess, sewing, gardening, dominoes, knitting, cooking and baking, dancing, arts and crafts. We had a "musical coffee house" for teens, as well as games, songs and stories for the little ones. And on it went. These volunteers all had different jobs but make no mistake; they were all on the same team.

The end result of all this effort? The juvenile crime rate dropped significantly. Kids were busy having fun and enjoying the attention while learning valuable life skills – including how to get along well with others.

Never hesitate to help one in need. Never underestimate the power of a loving act to heal both physically and spiritually.

As you reach out to your neighbor you accomplish great things. You do not enter into this work alone. Your prayer is heard and the help you need is at hand.

23 HELP YOURSELF TO MIRACLES

Make prayer your constant companion – your preoccupation.

It seems that "mini-miracles" are available to all who develop the habit of talking to God.

The Advisory Board of the Niagara Falls agency I was working for charged me with writing a grant proposal to gain funding for our youth-centered program. I was thoroughly intimidated because I had never written a proposal and didn't know how.

At the same time, a dear friend was struggling with multiple problems. Life for her was an uphill climb. As I learned more about her situation, I could understand why she believed she would be better off dead. Depression was the black cloud of her thinking. I kept in contact with her every day, praying for a change of heart. When I called to check on her at suppertime one day, she informed me that she was ready. She had formulated a plan, and knew how to take her life so that her children would not be the ones to find her body.

I acknowledged her statement and asked for one thing. "Let me pick you up and we will go somewhere to say a prayer together. I promise I will bring you right back home."

I knew of a tiny chapel at a local seminary. It was softly lit and we were alone, kneeling in front of the altar. Through anguish and tears she said repeatedly, "I'm so sorry." She seemed to be apologizing for making a mess of her life. I prayed aloud, asking God to work through her "right now" because she didn't believe she was a good person worthy of life. As the tears subsided she asked me to say a prayer with her. It was a prayer that a childhood girlfriend taught her, "The Memorare". She took special comfort in these words to Jesus' mother: "Never was it known that anyone who fled to thy protection, implored thy help or sought thy intercession was left unaided."

We said the prayer and left the chapel. In the car she heaved a sigh and said, "I feel so peaceful." The next day she connected with a counselor. The uphill climb from this point was to "a good life." She learned not to judge herself so harshly, and eventually went on to joyfully love and marry a man who was truly the light of her life.

While I was spending time with my friend, I was not working on the grant proposal. Facing a deadline, I was in a panic. I had heard about Charismatic prayer meetings at a local church but never attended one. I decided now was the time. I stood up and explained briefly about helping my friend and asked for a prayer of thanksgiving. Then I mentioned the proposal, not yet written, and my need for help from the Holy Spirit. The prayer and Biblical readings that followed were like an infusion of energy and inspiration. It was devout, reverent, and incredibly helpful to me.

 I got home about 9PM and sat down at the kitchen table with a yellow pad and a pencil that flew! By midnight, I had the nuts and bolts of the proposal all laid out and more than half completed. My request to God was for help getting it into the mail by the deadline. His response?

 It was chosen for funding and the program was a great success.

You are not powerless.

I am within you.

Yes, all of you.

24 POLITICS

Some politicians believe their responsibility is to their political party. One proposes legislation and the other (party) is committed to de-rail it. They out and out refuse to work together to find solutions to serious problems facing the nation.

When an election indicates a shift in political leadership, the majority blames the minority for every iota of the current problems, even if they were spawned last year or thirty years ago. Blaming does not lead to solutions. It cultivates greater bickering and dissension. Who can believe in leaders who refuse to lead?

Many in power are drunk with power and their decisions lack justice, compassion and love. Any government or organization that is divided against itself must fail. The people must demand better for themselves – for each other – for "survival". Humankind was not created by God for a life of misery or selfishness, war or greed. You were made for love, for compassion and creativity, for relationship and sharing, to lift each other up.

The Shame of the Nation
Jesus has strong words about the personal attacks and crass criticisms that candidates hurl at one another.

Leaders make fools of themselves as they try to make fools of their opponents in the election contest. Does anyone know what the "common good" is? Will the gigantic business interests dictate the rules of engagement that destroy the earth and the family of humankind? The ruthless war of words for votes is the shame of the nation.

Pray for wisdom and true charity (love) *in all those who govern and those who seek to govern. Pray for wisdom for all citizens that they will send good candidates to represent them in Washington and in every town hall. Those who abdicate responsibility* (to vote wisely) *will receive what they have sowed – nothing of substance.*

It's hard to avoid the daily barrage of news about political shenanigans by federal, state and local officials. It's painful to learn how Washington's corporate lobbyists use huge sums of money to entice "favors" from politicos. It's like rubbing salt into a wound to know that many politicians boost their retirement incomes by making deposits in foreign accounts. Shady practices are major and minor and legion. And through all of this, our middle class is shrinking and the poor are getting poorer.

The first presidential debate (Aug. 2015, Republican candidates) *was beyond absurd. Not a single question about wars – policy – energy - Iran - nuclear accord. No substance. Few politicians are on task. They are preening but not working for the common good. People wonder if they know what "the common good" is, or if they would recognize it if it stared them in the face.*

The problem looks insurmountable – and in human terms, it is. But the foundation of a solution is PRAYER. Prayer will open eyes and hearts that will recognize what's wrong. It will discern practical, do-able solutions, and it will find the people and the wherewithal to "fix" things.

In the past, I had strong opinions about politics and had a lot to say about current issues. But since I've been listening to "another voice," I save my breath. Jesus asks us to use our tools of prayer and love, just as He did when He was on earth.

As mentioned before…

THE TRULY URGENT NEED IS PRAYER. **Gathering an army of PRAY-ERS is a viable and realistic response to an impossible situation**. *It requires a multitude of willing people. Prayer is not an item on the national agenda, but it is the best hope for saving lives and coming to peace. Truly, it's time for us to storm heaven with our prayers.*

Can masses of us join or start a small prayer group and/or pray privately more frequently?

Time to Storm Heaven?

My good-natured father started to practice law in the late 1920s when Buffalo was a cluster of ethnic villages: Polish, Italian, German, African American, Irish, Hungarian and others. Many of his clients were immigrants who were struggling to learn a new language, so he understood their anxiety about dealing with legal problems.

When I was a child, there were many evenings when I heard him reassure clients who called on the telephone, telling them to get a good night's sleep while he did their worrying for them. We Americans would love to know that our elected officials were "doing the worrying" for us, and were working for the common good – trying their best to resolve our country's mega-problems.

Christ suggests that this "utopia" could be ours if enough of us storm heaven with our prayers. He asks us to pray more for our politicians, criticize them less, and do our best to vote wisely. He asks us to use love and compassion, just as He did when He was on earth. Jesus asks us to pray for those who make decisions that affect our lives because our prayer can create a difference, and can help our government function for the common good.

Pirates of Today

Those who battle over the budget will bring the USA to its knees. It's a case of the blind being elected by the blind. In their blindness, they fail to see their folly. They were sent to assure the population of the good for all citizens. Instead, they gave the keys of the vault to the robber barons of your time – like pirates who pillage and attack in order to guarantee their own security and luxury, but not the security of the whole population. The money lenders have money to burn, yet it will not keep them warm. The "group think" among the "haves" has turned brain into bone.

༄༅

Never pass by an opportunity to be kind and loving.

25 MATERIALISM

This may be the worst of the "-isms."

Does it register that MOST OF THE WORLD is destitute and hardly anyone notices? The consumption of the world's goods and resources by so few is proof that the blindness is almost total.

We Americans have unfettered access to fashionable clothing, vehicles, media devices, good food, prompt medical care, good housing and so on. We take it for granted. We don't even think about the poverty in our own cities and towns, much less our destitute brothers around the world.

More "Stuff" – Out of Control

Do you know how much materialism has separated the faithful from their Heavenly Father? They worship at the shrine of material goods. They even believe that material goods will bring them happiness. How wrong they are. For those who are caught up in materialism – more "stuff" is like a person dying of thirst eating salt.

The desire is great, but the fulfillment of the desire is impossible. True fulfillment comes from sharing what you have and extending love.

Greed is Greed

The description of the thirsty person is the microcosm of the corporations – especially the multinational corporations. No matter how they try to justify their actions, it is not possible today. Greed is greed no matter how you dress it. The PR people can spin tales, but the tales will hold up like cotton candy in a rainstorm. Please unite your prayers with the prayers of all, all over the world, who seek a just and loving and lasting Peace. The Prince of Peace will bless you.

Many good and faithful people have been sucked into the vortex of materialism. They may be our dear friends. They may be ourselves. We are easily attracted by the latest baubles, autos, shoes, clothing, media devices, and so on. Must our "Black Friday" splurge at the mall or the computer turn our attention from the birth of Jesus? Is there any money left for the local homeless mission? For the toy collections for poor families/children?

Know that your Heavenly Father created a world of plenty, a paradise, and today it is a composite of greed and envy for many. This is evidence of the worldwide decay. So many of the downtrodden are not even aware that the Kingdom belongs to them, too. This is not God's plan – it does not reflect His gifts to all humankind.

26   EXCLUDE NO ONE

Embrace Everyone

Embrace every country – every spiritual /religious group – every ethnic group. You don't have to make a judgment about who you should gather into your embrace and who is not worthy of your embrace. Sorting is not what you are asked to do. Know that the spark of the Divine is in everyone. Loving another does not mean loving another's decisions or behavior.

If people do not include the Spirit in their daily lives, if they do not treat others as they would like to be treated, disaster lies ahead.

Only One Family

Remember that all will return to their home together as one family. Learn to let go of all of the negativity of the past and present and embrace our family in love, for truly there is only one family.

My Dad, as a city judge in the 1950's and 1960's, had a strong sense of our unity and the value of each person. The examples we witnessed growing up were teaching moments for us, his six children.

One afternoon, he called my mother from City Court to tell her that he was bringing home a bereft woman with three little ones. They were homeless, hungry and tired. In the 1950's there were no shelters for battered women, no food stamps, no disposable diapers. I helped my mother prepare a meal for the family that the police had found in the back of a big truck. During the last two days, their only food had been a box of dry cereal.

It was a generous table that greeted them and the children ate like it might be their last meal. After they were fed and had fun splashy baths, life looked better. Dad put a big mattress on the floor next to a double bed so they would all be together through the night, and Mom made diapers by cutting up a soft old cotton quilt. Luckily, she had some of those big old diaper safety pins! Generous neighbors had some kids' clothes and cloth diapers to give them.

In two days, my Dad found them a place to stay and had the husband's wages garnisheed and the check sent to the mother. The Works of Mercy were real to our parents - so very real to us.

Help Each Other

Wake up. Be kind. Help each other. Feed each other. Offer shelter to the homeless. What you do unto others you do unto Me. Never forget that love begets love. It is an endless circle of good. It begets joy and the desire to reach out and help others. Carry this one step further and you will understand that you also help yourself. You will begin to feel the truth that all are one. There is unity in all life. Embrace the unity and feel the love that heals all separation. Love one another as I have loved you.

We can't all take strangers into our homes to sleep and eat, but we can still help by praying for them, and making an effort to contribute to, or volunteer at, one of the homeless shelters or food kitchens that pepper the American landscape. Christ asks us to see Him in everyone we meet.

So Much Divides Us

Many people are divided by politics and by religious beliefs. Some are divided by handicaps, and others by talent or lack of talent. Sports loyalties are divisive, and in extreme cases, all too common. And today, many of My brothers and sisters proclaim "Peace on earth; good will to humankind." Humankind must be willing to love – love neighbor as self. The peacemakers lead in teaching peace. A wave of change will remake the characteristics of humankind as each one teaches one by example.

Jesus laments the fact that too many families are divided by grudges – which are sometimes generational. Who hasn't heard this blunt old comment? "Carrying a grudge is like drinking poison and expecting the other person to die."

Find Me in Silence

In your oneness there is strength and there is

peace. You need both and you will find both in Me. You also need to set aside time for silence. In the silence you will find Me quite readily. I am always present, but you will not find communion with Me in the hub-bub of the daily grind.

Exclude No One

Praise all that is good in your life. Bless everyone. Exclude no one. It is now that people must recognize that unity is the only answer. All must know that humankind is one family and that family is united in the One God. I urge you again to review the gospels for inspiration and peace.

Avoid Disaster

It matters not what religion is professed or in what part of the world – if people do not include the Spirit in their daily lives – if they do not treat others as they would like to be treated – disaster lies ahead. You would not want this for your children and their children or any children anywhere.

27 IT'S NOT IMPOSSIBLE

Do not assume that miracles are difficult in situations that you perceive as difficult.
What appears to be impossible to you is not impossible to Me.

There were many times in my life when a coincidence was actually a "mini-miracle." What do you make of this one?

I walked into my kitchen one evening after returning from a class at Niagara University. My arms were full of books and folders. Jack sat at the table with our friend Dick, a father of six, who looked upset. His doctor had just told him that he could no longer work as a tile-setter because a calcium build-up in his elbow and shoulder joints was causing too much damage. He wondered how he was going to support his wife and children.

I couldn't believe it. The materials from my Education class on "Occupational Information" were just the ticket. I actually had the information he needed in my arms!

Use Your Power

I gave Dick the name and number of a counselor from the New York State Rehabilitation Office and explained how they could help him.

After testing, they recommended college for Dick and were able to pay a great deal of his tuition and expenses. His family pitched in and they scraped by with food stamps while he studied. Dick became a math teacher, and some years later, a Guidance Counselor.

It seemed that God gave us the answer even before we went to Him in prayer. It gave new credence to my favorite Unity Church prayer: "Let go and let God."

Our friendship with Dick continued, and several years later he mentioned yet another problem. He loved teaching and counseling. All was going well. But supporting a family of eight was still a challenge because at that time, teachers had no summer income. He received a call from the Niagara County Sheriff's office regarding a good summer job.

The first phase was to write a grant proposal for funding a "Dynamic Don't Drink and Drive" campaign. He didn't know how to write a proposal, but at this time I did, and I had a booklet with simple, easy-to-follow directions. When his writing was in process, he called me for a critique. Reading his work, it was clear that he not only understood proposal writing, he also had a deep understanding of the importance of making highway travel safer for everyone.

Proposals from around the state were reviewed over several months and Dick's became the model for New York State. He was called back to the Sheriff's office the following summer to begin implementation. Before long, he was offered a permanent position. Dick left his life as an educator in the school system and became a full time educator with a lifesaving curriculum.

28 BAD NEWS & GOOD NEWS

Media…media…media – it blankets our lives.

The masses are swayed from day to day with bits and pieces - "sound bites" - from one side or the other. The lessons of love that I came to share with humankind are not noticed in the avalanche of negative words and hostile thoughts that play all day in your media.

Those few who realize this pray sincerely for humankind. They understand that hostility, criticism, deceit, and anger are not the atmosphere that cultivates love. All the small groups that pray together each week must pray each day for peace and love to prevail. The alternative is unthinkable.

There was a time when I was a "news junkie," glued to TV talking heads that constantly fed us their network's version of current events. I had my own opinion on political issues and shared them with any willing listener. I read the daily newspaper, including editorial writers from across the country.

I do admire some outstanding TV commentators, guests, writers and producers who work to solve problems, to provide outstanding entertainment, to shine the light of "truth" on situations, and to bring people together in times of tragedy. But I often watched "empty" TV programs, too. I knew I needed more space for prayer and meditation and reading. I cut way back on watching TV.

Much of the "news" is gathered and censored by experts who decide what should be made available to you. Their "slant" on the news often misses My "slant."

I wrote this question in my notebook: "Jesus, why do we never see the sweat shops on the TV news that are the site of making our clothes or shoes and so many other consumer goods?" The labels tell us that most of our clothes are made by laborers in Bangladesh, Turkey, Sri Lanka, India and many more countries.

His response made me wince: *Look to "Big Business" for your answer. Production by slaves ensures great profit margins. That's the name of the game.*

I asked, "Is anyone trying to do anything about this?" His words were not encouraging:

*Those who are **doing** anything are the ones who are protecting the criminals. Pray for every* *person who lives in slavery. There are more than you can count. The feeling of aloneness and abandonment overwhelms them.*

The "news" cultivates division and dissension. That is their product. Turn to prayer. In the silence and peace you will hear me. Listen. The meandering mind is not productive of meditation and grace.

☙❧

When Paris erupted over the results of Charlie Hebdo's cartoons of the Prophet Mohammed, Jesus commented on the misuse of sarcasm toward a revered religious leader.

Making fun of religion - any religion - is not acceptable, and neither are planned attacks and executions. Those who resort to violence and murder as their "problem solving" method speak forcefully of their own lack of sanity.

At a meeting of sixty countries in June 2015 - an Anti-Extremism Summit - President Obama reminded all that Islam, in its truest expression, is a religion of peace. He made it clear that the USA takes issue with Muslim Extremists, not the dedicated Muslim people who are living, working and worshiping in our towns and cities everywhere.

Several of his comments:

- People get a distorted view of Islam because of the extremists.
- ISIS does not represent Islam.
- Respect people of every faith.
- Lift up voices of tolerance

The Good News
The news media has tremendous potential for cultivating a new society – a world of peace. Many in the media – writers, commentators, producers and directors, have worked tirelessly to solve problems, to bring people together in times of upheaval, to light a candle of hope when naysayers would blow it out.

How moving it was to see black and white Americans stand together in grief and solidarity after the horrendous massacre at Mother Emmanuel AME Church in Charleston, SC. And how comforting to hear President Obama's strong eulogy – ending with "Amazing Grace".

"The News" can chew up hours in a day. Christ confirmed this over and over when my TV would black out telling me to begin listening and scribing. There are many messages in my notebooks asking us to make time for meditation and prayer every day - to make it a top priority.

The US media is at the top of its game when publicity about American disasters or tragedies brings hundreds and hundreds of volunteers to stricken sites. They travel miles, roll up their sleeves and pitch in to help. I was proud of my niece Trish and her family for traveling to New Orleans during the flood of 2005. They were among the "saints" that "went marchin' in."

So many "good neighbors" showed up in South Carolina as soon as possible after their horrendous disaster from flooding and mud. These kinds of responses are part of America's soul. Millions KNOW that "we are our brother's keeper."

There are many examples of neighborly love as related in media (TV) stories. They are teaching moments for all. The peacemakers lead in teaching peace. A wave of change will remake the characteristics of Humankind – as each one teaches one, by example. Follow My example. My demonstrations of kindness, compassion and love. Learn to live by your principles, not by the latest news. Kindness, goodness and love are motivators. They are change agents of your time. This is change to believe in. Honor My birth with love. My love resides within you. Give it away every day to build peace.

29 TAKE A NEW LOOK

Remember the "Beatitudes"? Jesus referred to them many times in my scribing, and stressed their importance. For years, the Beatitudes left me with a lot of questions about just what they meant. But a relatively new Bible translation, *The Message*, helped clear them up for me - a casual translation:

- Blessed are the poor in spirit for theirs is the kingdom of heaven.
  You're blessed when you're at the end of your rope. Your prayers of love and hope will save you. You're blessed when there is nothing left but God, for then you are filled with God-life.

- Blessed are they who mourn for they shall be comforted.
  You're valued when you feel you've lost what or who is most dear to you. You will be embraced by the One most dear to you.

- Blessed are the meek; they shall inherit the earth.

    You are blessed when you're content with just who you are – no more, no less. That is the moment you find yourselves proud owners of everything that can't be bought.

- Blessed are those who hunger and thirst for righteousness, for they shall be filled.

    You're blessed when you've worked up a good appetite for serving God. You will be nourished by His unfailing Love.

- Blessed are the merciful for they shall obtain mercy.

    You are blessed when you care for others. At the moment of being "care-full" you will find yourself cared for.

- Blessed are the pure of heart for they shall see God.

    You're blessed when you get your inside world – your mind and heart – put right. Then you can see God in the outside world.

- Blessed are the peacemakers; they shall be called the children of God.

    You're blessed when you can show people how to cooperate, instead of compete or fight. That's when you discover who you

really are, and your place in God's family.

- Blessed are they who are persecuted for righteousness' sake for theirs is the kingdom of heaven.
  You are blessed when you are challenged for your beliefs in justice and love for all.

30 PRAY WITHOUT CEASING

Don't panic. Jesus doesn't mean we have to be on our knees 24/7. But He strongly urges us to weave mini-prayers into our daily lives. This, He assures us, can create a powerful shift in mankind's thinking. Over and over in the notebooks He urges you and me to *pray without ceasing.*

Pray for a change of heart for those who falsely believe that they are too busy for prayer.
When I ask you to pray unceasingly, I am asking you to think of humankind with a prayer in your heart. Offer your work and your activities for the good of all. Let your prayers be thoughts of blessing others. Leave no one out. **This could be the most important work you have ever done.** *All of humankind will benefit from your prayer.*

It's easy for me to take mini-breaks for prayer because as a child, I was "schooled" in the practice. Franciscan Sisters were our teachers in elementary school. The day began with prayer and the pledge to the flag. Before we walked home for lunch, Sister led us in the Guardian Angel prayer and reminded us to look both ways crossing the street. We said a prayer at the beginning and end of the afternoon session, too. "Special Intentions" were added almost daily. "My grandma is sick," "My cousin broke his arm." We never doubted that God heard our prayers.

Just Pray

The world is on the edge of destroying billions of people and planet Earth. Stop talking, and pray – as you drive, do laundry, travel, fix meals, take a lunch-break, do yard work or housework, and so on. Just pray. ***Pray with confidence.*** *A few whispered thoughts will do more good than you can imagine or calculate.* ***Never exclude anyone from your prayers.***

One snowy night my car started to slide into the next lane on the two-lane road. It wouldn't respond to the steering wheel. A big truck was coming down that lane and I shouted, "God help me!" My car slid over to the proper lane just in time.

Even before that, I had a habit of saying mini-prayers as I drove. Little snippets like: "God, be there for Joan's doctor appointment," "Thank you for helping John with his job interview," and so on. Falling asleep at night, the fleeting thought comes... "Jesus, thank you for the good of today, and help me to serve you tomorrow."

Can You See?

Set your daily intention of seeing goodness in others and doing good for others. I tell you, seeking material goods and ignoring your brothers and sisters in need are equivalent to telling your Heavenly Father that you have no time for His guidance in your life. Pray without ceasing for the conditions in the world. The blindness is ever growing and for many individuals numbness has set in. It is for those who can see to lead others in the path of love and justice.

After waking from sleep, try to remember to say a favorite phrase or affirmation such as, "I will to do your will today," or "Help me to see You in everyone I meet today." *Intention* enables us to "pray without ceasing."

Many people benefit from using a daily prayer booklet. They are available in pamphlet racks in churches, in religious stores, or through a quick trip to Google.

As more and more do this, they will come to know that rather than taking time from their busy schedule, they are adding peace and quality to their lives. Joy will follow.

I rely on many in the family of humankind to meet Me each day to pray and do good works to lift the whole of humankind. Consistency is needed and more workers in the vineyard are needed. Pray with Me each morning and when you can, connect with me in prayer in moments throughout the day.

F. deSales Kellick

Pray for those who think they are too busy for prayer.

31 PEACE - ANY HOPE?

I wrote this question in my notebook in early 2016: "Is my worry stronger than my faith about the possibility of peace? I need to do a lot of talking to myself about that."

Jesus' response:

One super power is not enough. There is no balance of power nor is there respect for the ultimate power. I speak of the power of God. The drumbeat of war is always present – at times obvious and loud. At other times it provides a background beat to discussion and negotiations that get nowhere but to the land of stress and mistrust. Children of God, wake up. All must be represented in the discussion that will seek peace for all. Peace is not a commodity that can be purchased by some and not by others. Humankind must purchase peace for all. It is not an item to be parceled out here and there

It is present for all or it is not peace. Many, many more must join those who actively seek peace through prayer. Prayer will change the mindset that believes war will solve the world's problems. Open your heart and mind to the possibility of peace. I speak to you as the Prince of Peace.

The Path of Conflict

Some attack with weapons – others with words. Both cause great pain. Accepting one another with honor and respect is foundational to the building of peace on earth. This is what humankind must seek in prayer. The urgency of this cannot be stated strongly enough. The world is in dire need of turning to God for help. All the events in the world arena are leading down the path of conflict. Lay down the guns and embrace each other in love and peace.

Radical Revolution Needed

A great revolution of love is needed *– a radical and wholehearted turning of people to love. There is ample evidence that conflict, hatred and war are not the answer to present day problems. They never were the answer. The Great Commandment defines the answer in simple terms that are understandable to all. "Love God with all your heart, mind, soul and strength, and love your neighbor as yourself." Carry these words with you throughout the day. They are the guide to peace – peace for all. You have calm and order in life when you adopt these words and apply them to every circumstance. Great companions are with you every moment of the day.*

The wars/conflicts take up all the space in newscasts. The Middle East, ISIS, refugees all over Europe – running away from persecution in their own country – people running for President who haven't a clue.

Just consider this – if all people were guided by the Corporal Works of Mercy, how many of these problems would still be taxing patience and making life intolerable? That's right. None of them.

*When people read our book it will shake a lot of them to the core. The simplicity of all this is astounding. It's not like you are being asked to explain the theory of relativity and all its implications. It's feed the hungry, visit the sick, give drink to the thirsty, visit the imprisoned (there are many kinds of prisons.) If only you would begin to notice "the other" and **do** something.*

I am in All ... you and all others. We are closer than you think. Tending to each other replaces the need to complain and make negatives the focus of your life. No wonder that so many are depressed. **Help someone. It will fill you with joy.**

In mid-2015, I wrote: ISIS announced that thousands may be held for execution. All of them are either Christian or Sunni. Dear Lord, what are we coming to? And Congress is fighting today about Homeland Security – fund it or not fund it? Seems like the adult version of a sandbox fight. Not all that rational.

No, it is not. And the question, "Am I my brother's keeper?" begs for an answer. The powerful ones revert to war and more war – and they are many. Others argue for peace – for meeting at the table and discussing the wisdom of de-escalation. Some of those with great power refuse to look at possibilities for peace. A few see peace – a workable peace – with all the players at the table – as the only alternative. Let your prayers for peace be continuous. Let your prayers shed light where there seems to be no light at all. **War is not the answer, prayer is.**

Addendum

A few days before the final submission of this book, I received the following from Jesus:

I am still the strong spiritual and compassionate presence that I have been for over two millennia. I ask you to be ready to tell others about your growing relationship with Me through your stories – your life experience. Speak of your life formation and your Mother's deep and unshakable faith. She was one who could preach eloquently without words – as you have noted in our book. Your father modeled this also – sometimes in the public courts.

Encourage others to pray, to be compassionate and forgiving. Apply this to personal life and to the critical situations around the world. The media presents these stories over and over again.

There are other stories – situations that you know nothing about – family conflicts, neighborhood "wars", military operations in various locations that seem to be a patchwork WW III.

And then there is world hunger – a massive mismanagement problem for all of humankind. All of these things and others demonstrate the dire need for prayer.

"Come to Me and I will refresh you" are not just empty words – they are words of reassurance. I want to help you and everyone who makes up the

human family.

The conflicts that are commonly referred to as the "problem of the Middle East" have tentacles that weave throughout countries – peoples – on every continent. Most people are unaware that the roots of all these problems are centuries deep.

They require forgiveness that is as deep and wide as the countless beings who have suffered and continue to suffer to this day. You can read or hear about some of them as the media spins their stories on front pages and TV screens.

Look all around you and all around the world. We speak of human beings in dire need of compassion and love - emotional as well as physical help - food and shelter, but also kindness and encouragement.

Though you cannot flit around the world to perform miracles of love, you can use the power of your prayer to do that for you. Everyone is your sister and brother. Everyone needs healing that is the product of love and forgiveness. Pray for peace.

END

About My Name (Everyone asks)

My mother took her nurse's training in the early 1900's at St. James Mercy Hospital in Hornell, NY. Sister Francis deSales was her favorite instructor and lifelong friend. So she named me, her fourth daughter, after the good Sister.

At age 3 or 4, I cringed when neighborhood kids called me "Franny" because it sounded too much like "fanny." So I announced to my little world that I was "deSales."

Turns out St. Francis deSales was born into French nobility in the Chateau de Sales. Because of his extensive writing he has become known as the patron of journalists. He wrote one of my favorite prayers. You may have seen it before:

"Do not look forward to what may happen to you tomorrow. The same everlasting Father who cares for you today, will care for you tomorrow and every day. Either He will shield you from suffering or He will give you unfailing strength. Be at peace then and set aside your anxious thoughts and imaginings."

My favorite one-liner from his writings:

"Be gentle with everyone, but first be gentle with yourself."

Acknowledgments – Many Thanks

I'm grateful to my "little sister" Dea, a wordsmith since childhood, for piecing together and organizing so many parts of my treasured notebooks for publication. I even forgive her now for "disappearing" on Saturday mornings at home when it was our turn to each scrub one-half of the huge kitchen floor.

During the process, various writer-friends of hers came with sharp minds and pencils to smooth out any bumps in the manuscript. They made good calls all the time. Our God-Squad included Pat McClain, Dianne Riordan, Lorene Duquin, Evelyn Brady, Tom O'Malley, Annie Lienert, as well as Irene Filbin and Nancy Reynolds Eidt (recently deceased). Jesus actually reminded me of the equal value of those who came to the vineyard late. Their help was essential to the need. Friends Michelle Montour and Nancy Geiser were right there when we needed a computer expert to untangle our glitches.

And I can't forget Dea's dear Tom Wagner (USMC) for his patience through this long process. His humor and lightheartedness kept us perking along.

A heartfelt thanks to my "Tuesday Night Prayer Group" – a warm and steady support during my years of scribing.

As far as I'm concerned, all of the above are Angels.

Appendix

In addition to the Bible, some of the readings Jack and I shared included: Emmet Fox (he led us to the psalms), Charles Fillmore, Meister Eckhart, Abraham Joshua Heschel, the life of St. Teresa of Avila, St. John of the Cross, Theresa the Little Flower of Jesus, and material from the Unity Village Press in Missouri.

Readings of my own include these writers:

Thomas Merton, Pierre Teilhard de Chardin, *A Course in Miracles* scribed by Helen Schucman, Hildegard of Bingen, Albert Nolan, J. Krishnamurti, Caroline Myss, Wayne Dyer, the Diary of St. Maria Faustina Kowalska, the Dalai Lama, Esther deWaal, Pope Francis, Hugh Brady, Jean Vanier, Elaine Pagels, Margaret Schlacta SSS, Max Lucado, Marcus Borg, Joseph Goldstein, Desmond Tutu, Karen Armstrong, Thich Nhat Hanh, Idries Shah, William Johnson, Diarmuid O'Merchu, Walter Kasper, Gary Zukov, John Dominic Crossan, Andrew Harvey, Kahlil Gibran, Joseph Girzone, and Luke Timothy Johnson.

Made in the USA
Middletown, DE
21 July 2016